ENGLAND
FROM THE AIR

ENGLAND
FROM THE AIR

Annabel Walker

Foreword by John Timpson

Harry N. Abrams, Inc., Publishers, New York

For my Parents

Library of Congress Cataloguing-in-Publication Data

England from the air / [compiled by] Annabel Walker.
  p.   cm.
  ISBN 0–8109–0894–8
  1. England—Aerial photographs. 2. England—
Description and travel—1971—
—Views. I. Walker, Annabel.
DA667.E4925 1988
914.2'0022'2—dc19   88–14717

Published in 1989 by Harry N. Abrams,
Incorporated, New York

A Times Mirror Company

Designed by Joy FitzSimmons

Map by Line on Line

Printed and bound in Italy

Half title page *Alkborough, Humberside*
Title page *Belvoir Castle, Leicestershire*
Above *Blackpool, Lancashir*e

FOREWORD
by John Timpson

Each time I flew home from a BBC assignment abroad it was a marvellous moment to cross the English coast and look down on that familiar and much-loved patchwork of green and brown and gold – familiar, much-loved, yet so difficult to identify. Unless the captain told us, I was never sure whether I was hovering over Hampshire, swooping over Sussex, or cruising over Kent.

There might be a glimpse of a great cathedral. I could not tell if it was Chichester or Canterbury. There might be a length of motorway. Was it the M20 to Maidstone or the M23 to Pease Pottage? And as we circled over the London suburbs, might that patch of green south of the river be Putney Heath or Kew Gardens? Was that intricate pattern of semidetached houses Wealdstone or Wembley Park? And those large sheets of water squared off at the corners, they must be the reservoirs at Staines – but if they are, we ought to be landing by now . . .

In short, I am quite hopeless at recognizing places from the air. I find it slightly easier now I can use Norwich Airport, where the aeroplanes fly lower and slower. As there is only one city within fifty miles, I can even recognize Norwich Cathedral. But what a treat to be able to linger over the photographs in this book, to study in detail so many familiar landmarks from such an unfamiliar angle – and to recognize correctly what I had identified quite wrongly before.

That little park just off St James's, for instance, with the block of buildings round a quadrangle at one end, now I know that is the Queen's private garden behind Buckingham Palace. Those four high rectangles by the Thames, a layout not unlike a prison, with an exercise yard in each rectangle, were built as a hospital, not a prison; it is now the Royal Naval College at Greenwich. And now that I can look down on the City at my leisure, instead of glimpsing it briefly through the window before we banked and it turned into sky, I can pick out – with a little guidance from Annabel Walker's text – those ostentatious symbols of banking wealth, the Barclay Tower, which is quite big enough, and the National Westminster, which is even bigger.

But this book serves not only to enlighten and inform, and sometimes surprise. Its photographs are worth studying in their own right; they are a delight to the eye. Take the Needles, giant chips of rock escaping from the cliff and heading purposefully out to sea, led by a little red and white lighthouse, or Lake Coniston, embodying three different aspects of the Lake District – the densely wooded shores of the lake itself, the low-lying fields in the foreground, the bare grandeur of the mountains in the distance – all contained in a single photograph, or Robin Hood's Bay, a cluster of cottages on the hillside with just a single narrow street leading down to the harbour, making me quite certain at first sight it was Clovelly.

I have much enjoyed this aerial tour of England. I shall enjoy it even more when the captain announces, 'If you look through the windows on the right you will see . . .' and I shall cry, 'I know!'

INTRODUCTION

The variety of the English landscape is enormous and endlessly fascinating, from marshland to mountains, from plains that are flat as a pancake to undulating country with hardly a level site for miles around. There are wooded areas and desolate ones; some have been influenced by the hand of man for centuries, and others man has left alone. And there is no better way to see that landscape than from the air.

Flying above England is like a variation on one of those fairy-tales in which the toys in the playroom, or the figures in a painting, spring to life. The maps over which one has so often pored are suddenly revealed in three dimensions; in place of small black dots and coloured contour lines are real houses and hills, exactly where the maps said they were, but looking utterly different.

All those geography lessons about the three stages of a river's course, or the crumpling of rock in gigantic upheavals, are translated into physical realities. The exquisite designs of the great Georgian landscape architects can be appreciated from the air in a way that none of their owners could enjoy; traces of lost villages and obsolete farming patterns still show through the cultivations of later centuries; patterns made by the sea on sand and rock can be clearly seen.

The aerial view does distort and dissemble too. It eliminates hills, particularly in urban settings, so that one is led to imagine that places are much more level than they are: the photographs of Bristol (page 54) and Kinder Scout (page 84) are just two examples. And it happily ignores much of the mess with which we humans surround ourselves. Even a vast urban sprawl appears to be a simple mixture of bricks, concrete and a little greenery; small, relatively unspoilt country towns look as though they have been scrubbed clean. Litter and minor untidiness do not show up when they are a thousand feet below the camera.

Perhaps that is why aerial photographs are so attractive. The clean lines and lovely colours are very easy on the eye, especially where the subject matter is simple and straightforward. Castles and coastlines in particular are appealing – it would have been easy to fill the entire book with pictures of these.

Ultimately, however, a view of the English landscape is a history of its people. There are very few places on this small island that have not been affected by the activities of man – though there are photographs in this book of one or two such places. The rocks of the Needles and Old Harry, for example, have been changed over the centuries, but only by the sea. The mountain peaks of the Lake District are beyond the reach of farmers; and a number of rivers pursue their courses as they always have done, though the country through which they flow has probably altered radically over the years.

Most views of England, however, are of a landscape at least partly man-made. This is self-evident in built-up areas, but is also true of the countryside. The idea that 'the country' is a timeless place, where hedgerows have always flourished and sheep have always grazed, is simply not correct.

Many of those hedgerows have been in existence only since the enclosures of the eighteenth century. Sheep have been raised in certain parts of the country for many centuries, in others they are a comparatively recent introduction. Two hundred years may seem a long time, but it is a relatively short period in the history of farming, and a mere breath compared with the ages through which the underlying geological structure of England has been forming.

It is fun to potter through lanes looking at the countryside, or wander through towns trying to piece together their development; but the view from the ground is always limited. If, for example, you want to understand the medieval plan of Warkworth (page 107), you can walk along the high street, and then along the back street, and then study the map. But the aerial photograph of that delightful little town shows you in an instant how it was arranged and divided into plots.

Any choice of photographs from the vast collection of Aerofilms Ltd is bound not to be comprehensive. There are thousands of pictures in their library at Borehamwood in Hertfordshire from which to choose, and one is only too aware in making a selection that many places have to be left out. We have tried to cover the ground fairly evenly; but we have also wanted to depict the variety of England and of its counties, in differing weather conditions and at all seasons. There are famous areas of outstanding beauty to be shown, there are cities and industries, and there are the quieter places, all of which make England the extraordinary, densely worked patchwork quilt that it is.

ACKNOWLEDGEMENTS

This book could not have been produced without the help of Peter O'Connell or Michael Willis at Aerofilms who guided us through shelf after shelf of files and archives. Thanks must also go to Dr Lunn at the Extra-Mural Studies department of Newcastle University, D. J. Lyon, head of enquiry services at the National Maritime Museum, and to information and press officers at Heathrow, All England Lawn Tennis and Croquet Club, Associated British Ports, Buckingham Palace, the Bluebell Railway Preservation Society, the Open University, Didcot Power Station and the CEGB, Warwick Castle, Anglian Water, Granada Television, the Greater Manchester Museum of Science and Industry, English Estates, the town councils of Scunthorpe, Consett, Gillingham and Berwick-upon-Tweed, Harwich library and the city councils of York and Norwich. Among the many kind friends who have taken an interest in this book, Alex Roe, Ned Boyd, Francis Machin and Andrew Grant helped with specific photographs; and Felicity Luard, Managing Editor at George Weidenfeld and Nicolson, showed unfailing patience and helpfulness from start to finish.

SCOTLAND

NORTH SEA

NORTHERN IRELAND

IRISH REPUBLIC

IRISH SEA

WALES

NORTH SEA

ENGLISH CHANNEL

Ladies Skerrs
Bucket Rocks
Holy Island
Bamburgh
Warkworth

NORTHUMBERLAND

Hadrian's Wall
Tynemouth
Newcastle upon Tyne
TYNE AND WEAR
Consett
CUMBRIA
Bishop
Auckland
Durham
High Force
Teesmouth
CO DURHAM
Derwent Fells
CLEVELAND
Robin Hood's Bay
Sea Fell
Barnard
Bowness
Castle
Coniston
Water
NORTH YORKSHIRE
Bortree Tarn

ISLE OF MAN
Laxey
Fountain's
Abbey
Castle Howard
Castletown
Isle of
Walney
Lancaster
Malham Cove
York
Glusburn
HUMBERSIDE
Hotham
Blackpool
LANCASHIRE
Humber Bridge
WEST YORKSHIRE
Spurn Head
Emley Moor
GREATER
MANCHESTER
SOUTH
YORKSHIRE
Scunthorpe
Manchester
Cown Edge Rocks
Willoughton
MERSEYSIDE
Kinder Scout
West Burton
Liverpool
River
Lose Hill
Widnes
Bollin
Lincoln
CHESHIRE
DERBYSHIRE
Beeston
Peckforton
Stoke-on-Trent
NOTTINGHAMSHIRE
Colston
Bassett
LINCOLNSHIRE
Cley next the Sea
STAFFORDSHIRE
Belvoir
Sandringham
LEICESTERSHIRE
The Wrekin
Tamworth
Edith
Stamford
Norwich
Park
Weston
Burghley House
Much Wenlock
Wolverhampton
Rockingham
SHROPSHIRE
WEST MIDLANDS
Ely
Birmingham
NORTHAMPTONSHIRE
Southwold
WORCESTERSHIRE
Bury St Edmunds
Warwick
Whiston
Cambridge
HEREFORD AND
WORCESTER
Madresfield Court
Milton
Felixstowe
Malvern Hills
Malvern
Keynes
Ampthill
Saffron
Harwich
Walden
Stow-on-the-Wold
River
Symonds Yat
GLOUCESTERSHIRE
Dunstable
Blackwater
Lower
Oxford
Maldon
Slaughter
OXFORDSHIRE
ESSEX
Severn Bridge
Didcot Power
River Thames
Station
Windsor
Osterley
Henley
LONDON
AVON
Bristol
BERKSHIRE
Heathrow
Hampton
Bath
Court
River Medway
WILTSHIRE
Weybridge
Westbury
SURREY
Leeds Castle
White Horse
KENT
Cheddar Gorge
Wells
Stonehenge
St Margaret's at Cliffe
Quantock Hills
HAMPSHIRE
Haslemere
Dover
SOMERSET
Glastonbury Tor
Old Sarum
WEST SUSSEX
Bluebell Line
Salisbury
EAST SUSSEX
Speke's Mill Mouth
Sherborne
Chichester
Brighton
Southampton
DORSET
Breamore
Beachy Head
DEVON
Maiden
Poole
Cowes
Portsmouth
River Camel
Launceston
River Exe
Castle
Old Harry
The
ISLE OF WIGHT
Calstock
Dartmoor
Rocks
Needles
Restormel
Castle
Plymouth
River
CORNWALL
Erme
Plymouth
Dartmouth
Thurlestone
Rock
St Anthony
Head

ST PAUL'S CATHEDRAL, London

No matter how hemmed in by modern buildings, St Paul's Cathedral still stands out in its splendour. Built to the designs of Sir Christopher Wren after the Great Fire of 1666 had destroyed the earlier cathedral, in those days it dominated its surroundings. During the Second World War when the area was again devastated it survived the bombs, only to be insulted by the antics of post-war planners, architects and builders who surrounded it with ugly monolithic blocks. St Paul's was once the dominant feature in a City landscape sprinkled with Wren spires; now it is only from one or two vantage points that one can enjoy the sight of it relatively unobscured by the bulk of modern office towers. There is a chance, however, that the cathedral might gain a few better-looking neighbours since Paternoster Square, to the left of the cathedral in this picture, is due for demolition and rebuilding. The Prince of Wales leads the fight to ensure that what goes up this time does not repeat the mistakes of the 1950s and 1960s.

THE CITY, London

This is the City of London, one of the leading financial centres in the world. Over the centuries it has grown, burnt down and grown again. The result is a fantastic combination of the monumental and the diminutive, the banal and the futuristic. Here the huge black glass buildings dominate: they are the Commercial Union and P & O buildings at the junction of Bishopsgate and Leadenhall Street. To the right, with blue cranes in its roof, is the new Lloyds building, designed by Richard Rogers. In the bottom right-hand corner of the photograph is the Barclays Bank tower, and on the far left, only half in the picture, is London's tallest building, the National Westminster Tower (due to be overtaken by the proposed tower at Canary Wharf in Docklands). At the very top left-hand corner is Spitalfields Market, London's historic vegetable market, which is shortly to be moved to another site. Among these extravagant new buildings the church spires that originally formed the City skyline are just visible, almost submerged in a sea of glass and concrete.

11

THE TOWER, London

The Tower of London has played a central part in the history of England since it was built by William the Conqueror soon after his arrival in 1066. It has welcomed monarchs on their triumphal way to coronation, and it has witnessed their deaths. It has sheltered the Crown Jewels since 1303, and it has imprisoned both the guilty and the innocent. There was a royal menagerie here for centuries, but in the 1830s the animals were moved to what is now London Zoo, and only the ravens remain. Tower Bridge is almost as famous as the tower itself, yet its history is very much shorter. There was no bridge here at all until the 1890s when it was opened by the Prince of Wales, later King Edward VII; since then its great steel-and-stone bulk has dominated the river. There is a high-level footbridge above the main span of the bridge for those who do not suffer from vertigo, and the view from the top is marvellous. Until very recently there were only disused docks to look at immediately downstream of the bridge, but in the 1970s old St Katharine's Dock began to be refurbished and has now become a fashionable tourist attraction.

DOCKLAND, London

This panoramic view east along the Thames gives a good idea of the extent of London's old dockland. Nowadays, of course, the docks are much farther downstream and this area changes weekly as it is transformed into the capital's most talked-about new residential area. In the foreground is Wapping, running into Limehouse, with Surrey Docks on the southern bank. Then comes the peninsula of the Isle of Dogs where the Thames makes a sudden, sharp southern loop; then in the far distance the Royal Victoria and Royal Albert Docks, where the new City airport has been built. If current plans are put into effect, the huge tower of Canary Wharf will soon make a further change to the landscape where the old West India Docks lie at the top of the Isle of Dogs. This part of London was once an area of isolated hamlets, but in the early nineteenth century its metamorphosis began with the opening of the first docks, and by the 1860s it had become a seething, overcrowded and poverty-stricken place, the atmosphere of which Dickens brilliantly conveyed in *Oliver Twist* and *Our Mutual Friend*. In the present century the slums were cleared and replaced with council blocks, and the docks were closed in 1980.

BUCKINGHAM PALACE, London

This is a view that many a tourist longs to see. The east front of Buckingham Palace is on permanent display, but high walls and tall trees keep its gardens a secret – except from aeroplanes. The grounds extend to forty-five acres, and most of the time they are a peaceful haven for royalty and wildlife. Every summer, however, they are visited by thousands of people when the Queen holds her garden parties. Surrounding thoroughfares grind to a halt while guests flood in from all over the country. Buckingham Palace has in fact been the monarch's residence for a relatively short time. Kensington Palace served that purpose for many years until King George IV decided in the 1820s to have his father's old home, Buckingham House – so called because it had been bought from the Duke of Buckingham – transformed at vast cost into a palace designed by John Nash. The work took far longer than had been estimated and was not completed until after Queen Victoria came to the throne. Even then, the palace did not look as it does today, because it gained its now familiar east façade of Portland stone only in 1913.

GREENWICH, London

London has surprisingly few great 'set pieces', and therefore the symmetry and dignity of the Royal Naval College at Greenwich stand out in the capital. An aerial view shows off the grand plan of the college and the park behind it, though it disguises the fact that it is quite a steep climb to the avenue of trees at the top. The park was laid out in the 1660s when King Charles II was planning to build himself a palace here. But he never finished his project, and it was not taken up again until the 1690s when a hospital for seamen was built to designs by Sir Christopher Wren. An avenue had to be created at its centre to preserve the view to the river of the Queen's House, the smaller white house that had been begun in 1616 by Inigo Jones for the wife of King James I. Nowadays these beautiful buildings house a training college for naval officers and the National Maritime Museum. The Royal Observatory on the hill behind the college is the building through which the Greenwich Meridian passes, and nearby is another museum, once the home of John Flamsteed, the first Astronomer Royal.

OSTERLEY PARK, Greater London

The low winter sun casts long shadows across Osterley Park, on the western edge of London. This estate lay in deep countryside when its first house was built here in Elizabethan times, and even in the early years of the present century it enjoyed a rural setting. But roads and railways have brought the inevitable rash of 'little boxes' with them and now the park is surrounded by houses. The M4 motorway cuts through it to the north of the house and aircraft fly over it night and day on their way to and from Heathrow Airport, just four miles to the west. All the same, the park and house still have an air of tranquillity that is no doubt appreciated by all those who visit them – by courtesy of the National Trust, which owns Osterley now. The house in its present form is the result of remodelling between 1761 and 1780 by Robert Adam. It still possesses the furniture that he also designed for its owners, the banking family of Child. The old stable block and kitchen garden are all that remain of the earlier buildings.

HAMPTON COURT PALACE, Greater London

On the banks of the Thames a few miles south-west of central London stands Hampton Court Palace, a magnificent building combining Tudor with William and Mary architecture. The combination shows up clearly in this aerial view: the palace appears Tudor from the entrance by the bridge, but classical from the south front. The site was first chosen for a house by Thomas Wolsey, Cardinal and Lord Chancellor, in c. 1515; after Wolsey's fall and death, his royal master King Henry VIII took over the palace and extended it, at the same time trying to erase reminders of its former owner. Queen Elizabeth I also spent much time here, taking particular interest in the gardens where she planted tobacco and potatoes brought from America. Sir Christopher Wren extensively rebuilt the palace for William and Mary, who did not care for Whitehall where the damp air exacerbated the king's asthma. Had it not been for the queen's death and limited funds, Wren might have had the entire palace demolished. As it was, only the Tudor state apartments came down, and the splendid buildings of Fountain Court went up in their place. The palace has not been the home of royalty since the days of King George II.

HEATHROW AIRPORT, Greater London

At the moment that this photograph was taken there were thousands of people milling about inside Heathrow's four terminals. Between 31 and 32 million passengers pass through the airport in a year, the equivalent of about 86,000 every single day, and there are more than 47,000 airport employees on site. Heathrow is the busiest international airport in the world, linking directly with 200 destinations all over the world. This unfamiliar view of it is taken from the north-east and shows Terminal One in front of the control tower and, beyond that, the cargo terminals and the reservoirs of the Staines area.

WIMBLEDON, London

This picture of the All England Tennis and Croquet Club at Wimbledon was taken during the 1987 championship, when Pat Cash won the men's singles, and Martina Navratilova triumphed again in the women's singles. Over the thirteen days of the championship no fewer than 395,823 spectators walked through the gates to watch matches played on the club's eighteen grass courts. The very first Wimbledon Championship took place back in 1877, forty-five years before the club moved to its present ground here in Church Road, and there is now a Lawn Tennis Museum here too, charting the history of the game from those early days. The game of croquet was initially the more important of the two games, but it was soon overshadowed by tennis to the extent that the full title of the club is often forgotten by the public. Croquet is still played and there is an annual tournament for club members.

HASLEMERE, Surrey

Haslemere lies at the south-western tip of Surrey, on the borders of both Hampshire and Sussex – but is no less characteristic of the county for all that. Surrey may be overrun by suburbia at its northern fringes where it abuts London, but farther south there are still great stretches of woodland and sandy hills, and towns such as Haslemere that proclaim their historic independence from the capital. This little place was already a town in the fourteenth century, and later benefited from the ironworks that were once widespread throughout Sussex and parts of Surrey. This is the heart of the town, the building marooned on its island being the town hall, which was built in 1814. Haslemere's conversion to a residential centre firmly linked to London began in Victorian times, when it became popular with several writers. Tennyson built himself a house in the 1860s, just beyond the town on Blackdown (the house is now owned by the National Trust), and died there in 1892. Another literary figure who lived, albeit briefly, in the area was Mary Ann Evans, known to her reading public as George Eliot. She rented a house in the summer of 1871 while working on her great novel *Middlemarch*.

WEYBRIDGE, Surrey

This is Weybridge in watery northern Surrey. The land here is covered with ponds and reservoirs and rivers and streams. At Weybridge the River Wey joins the Thames as it makes a few last little twists and turns before settling into the great sweeps that take it down through London to the sea. It is not surprising that the town is a popular place for commuters to the city: apart from the fact that it is on a main railway line that has made it easily accessible since the mid-nineteenth century, it has the magnetic attraction of water. So many people love a riverside – though it is not everyone who would want to live on an island whose only link with the mainland was a boat. There are plenty of alternatives in Weybridge, however, including the exclusive St George's Hill and Oatlands estates, which make it one of the most 'desirable' places in London's stockbroker belt.

CHICHESTER, West Sussex

Chichester is a charmingly English cathedral town but, all the same, it is different from other such places, for it has the scent of the sea about it. The town is not on the coast, but it is not far from it, and yachts and dinghies pepper the shores of Chichester Harbour. Chichester was one of the earliest cities in Britain to be built by the Romans, who called it Noviomagus; traces of their original city wall survive. The cathedral was built early in the twelfth century and has had a rather chequered history, burning down twice, being attacked during the Civil War and partly collapsing in 1861. Its detached bell tower is unique in England, and its spire is a landmark for miles around; indeed Chichester itself is rather a landmark in that it sits just at the point where the hills of the South Downs

give way to flat coastal land east of the harbour. The market cross, which stands at the junction of the town's main streets, was built by the bishop in 1500 and in later times there rose around it some delightful Georgian buildings.

BLUEBELL LINE, East and West Sussex

The delightfully named Bluebell Line is a diminutive section of railway track that was rescued by a group of admirers when British Rail closed the old East Grinstead to Lewes line in 1959. Now trains run purely for the pleasure of anyone who likes to see the five miles between Sheffield Park and Horsted Keynes from the windows of the carriages. There is a full-time staff of twelve, and also lots of

volunteers who help to keep the trains running – including part-time voluntary drivers. All the engines and rolling stock come from the old Southern Railway and its constituent companies and are of different ages, from thirty to over a hundred years old. The line is open all year round, and crosses the boundary between East and West Sussex a short distance from Sheffield Park, where the beautiful gardens – sadly battered by the great storm of October 1987 – are owned by the National Trust. Within the next ten years the preservation society hopes to extend the line a further six miles beyond Horsted Keynes to link up with the main network at East Grinstead.

BEACHY HEAD, East Sussex

Beachy Head is a famous landmark in England and a popular place with comedians for the imaginary disposal of mothers-in-law. Its great white, chalk cliffs are characteristic of this part of the coastline, and are particularly significant to all those who remember how threatened the entire Sussex coast was in the early years of this century. As transport improved, and since farming was suffering lean times, farmland along the cliffs became sprinkled with bungalows and shacks that threatened to cover the entire coastal countryside from Chichester to Dover. Fortunately, conservationists managed to prevent that happening. England has eyesores on its coastline as it has inland, but it also has miles of unspoilt cliffs and seashore.

BRIGHTON, East Sussex

Who knows what Brighton would be like today had King George IV not decided to have a house built there in the early 1800s. The little fishing village – known as Brighthelmstone until the nineteenth century – had already attracted a certain amount of attention as a suitable spot for sea bathing, but it was the creation of George IV's Royal Pavilion that gave the impetus to the building of the elegant terraces and crescents for which it is now famous. George was still Prince Regent when in 1815 he commissioned his favourite architect, John Nash, to transform a farmhouse into an Indian palace with a Chinese interior. He had already commissioned and abandoned Carlton House in London, begun hugely expensive work on Buckingham Palace, and made major alterations to Windsor Castle – and his interest waned in the new Pavilion as soon as it was created. Not surprisingly, the public disapproved of the king's extravagance, and when George IV died in 1830, Nash's career died with him. But the Pavilion remains and can be seen here in the centre of the picture.

SOUTHAMPTON DOCKS, Hampshire

Southampton is the country's largest importer and exporter of new vehicles, handling 200,000 in 1987. Here at the Prince Charles Container Port, neatly ordered rows of Fiat cars are awaiting distribution across the country from the vehicle import terminal of World Shipping and Freight Limited. Next door, on the corner of the dock, is British Telecom International's marine cable terminal – the cable drums can be seen lined up to the right of the building. To the right again is the berth of Southampton Container Terminals Ltd, the largest single-berth operation in the country in terms of throughput, handling 325,000 containers in 1987. And all this is just one corner of Southampton's busy docks. This is the south coast's premier port and a leading exporter of grain, shipping out more than 1 million tonnes each year. It is also, of course, a ferry terminal for France and the Isle of Wight and, although its liner traffic has declined, Southampton remains Britain's main port in this respect and cruises continue to be popular.

HMS VICTORY, PORTSMOUTH DOCKYARD, Hampshire

This is the stout little ship in which Nelson sailed to Trafalgar in 1805, HMS *Victory*. Compared with the gigantic tankers that ply the seas today she seems more like a scale model than the real thing. She was a useful vessel in her time, however, serving several admirals as their flagship. In 1797 she became a prison hulk at Chatham, where she might eventually have succumbed to decay had Admiral Nelson not noticed her and rescued her for his own use. It was on her deck that he met his end; surely one of the most famous deaths in British history.

PORTSMOUTH HARBOUR, Hampshire

Portsmouth has been a harbour of major importance for centuries. This great stretch of landlocked water is sheltered from the sea by the Isle of Wight and is large enough to hold the entire British fleet. Its qualities were recognized early; in the Middle Ages it became a dockyard and later it grew to be Britain's greatest naval base. Now the Navy has reduced its presence in Portsmouth, and ferry services to France are threatened by the construction of the Channel Tunnel. But Portsmouth may well survive in a different guise as a centre for leisure activities and water sports in a new age of recreation.

BREAMORE, Hampshire

Of all the traditional buildings in the English countryside, none is more serene than the parish church. Serenity is in its purpose, in its age, and in the harmony it enjoys with the surrounding landscape. This church, dedicated to St Mary, is at Breamore (pronounced Bremmer) and is one of the oldest surviving in the country: all its main walls are Saxon and there is an Old English inscription over one of its arches which reads 'Here the covenant is manifested to you.' Saxon churches are rare survivals – most were built of wood, and even stone ones were often replaced by the Normans after the invasion of 1066 – so Breamore is an important building, as well as a charming one, lying amid tranquil meadows on the northern edge of the New Forest.

THE NEEDLES, Isle of Wight

The Needles may be one of the most familiar sights in England but their extraordinary appearance ensures that they are always eyecatching, especially in dramatic photographs such as this. Here is the tail end of a ridge of chalk that stretches across the Isle of Wight from east to west dividing it in two. On the east coast it meets the sea at Culver Cliff. Here at the Needles it disappears under the sea, to reappear at the cliffs of the Isle of Purbeck (see page 33). Aeons of the washing of the sea around this point has isolated ridges that are well known to everyone who has sailed in and out of Southampton along the Solent. Far away along the coast of the island is Cowes, with Yarmouth rather nearer, beyond the most prominent point. The mainland of Hampshire can also be seen on the left.

COWES, Isle of Wight

Despite all the jokes about its name, the small town of Cowes on the Isle of Wight has thoroughly sensible origins, being called after the two 'cows' or forts built at the mouth of the River Medina by King Henry VIII as defences against foreign aggressors. These days Cowes welcomes hordes of visitors each August when it is the scene of a series of regattas, an event popularly known as Cowes Week. The water teems with boats and the narrow streets of old Cowes teem with people. There are parties and dances galore, and sometimes even the weather is fine. The racing tradition dates from 1826, when the Royal Yacht Squadron first organized races among its members. At other times of the year Cowes is a quieter place, though its boatyards, wharves and marinas keep its attention focused on the sea. It has been building boats since the reign of Elizabeth I, and now it builds hovercraft too. This view is taken looking north down the Medina to the Solent, with the Hampshire shore and the entrance to Southampton Water in the distance.

POOLE HARBOUR, Dorset

Poole Harbour is only about seven miles long, but its wandering shoreline and mazy inlets mean that its periphery measures about 100 miles. It is bordered on its eastern edge by the town of Poole, which has expanded rapidly in recent years. But on the west there are still miles of heathland and, in the distance, the Purbeck Hills. In the harbour itself lie numerous islands, most of them tiny; Brownsea is by far the largest, as this picture shows. It covers 500 acres and is now a nature reserve, but in 1907 it was the scene of Baden-Powell's first experimental camp for the scout movement. Poole Harbour is a fine expanse of water and was once a great centre of trade: merchants dealing with Newfoundland based themselves here, and many of Newfoundland's early settlers originated in this part of Dorset. Today the harbour is a haven for dinghy sailors, sheltered from the sea by this spit of land, which is known appropriately as Sandbanks. There is a new interest in the geology of the area, however, and that is the discovery of oil, which has led to friction between the oil companies and conservationists over the preservation of Dorset's precious heathland.

OLD HARRY ROCKS, Dorset

The chalk cliffs and detached rocks of the Foreland (or Handfast Point) on the Isle of Purbeck point eastwards across the sea towards their more famous cousins, the Needles off the Isle of Wight (see page 30). That is no coincidence, for they are part of the same edge of an inclined bed of chalk that runs across the Isle of Wight and then under the sea until it re-emerges here in Dorset. The sea has carved it into the clean lines of these cliffs and the little wedge-shaped headlands and pillars. The detached lumps are known as Old Harry Rocks (Old Harry being, of course, the Devil); the last stack is called Old Harry's Wife.

33

SHERBORNE, Dorset

The character of Sherborne in Dorset is shaped
by the presence in its midst of an abbey church
and a historic school, both built of beautiful
golden stone from nearby Ham Hill in
Somerset. The abbey is in the foreground, with
the school's 'great court' behind. The profusion
of ecclesiastically inspired buildings gives the
place a medieval air that is all too rare in
English towns today, battered as they so often
have been by twentieth-century planners.
Schooling in Sherborne goes back a long way,
having started in 705 under the direction of the
church. King Edward VI refounded it as a
grammar school, and in Victorian times it was
greatly enlarged by the headmaster of the day,
the Reverend H.B. Harper. More buildings went
up as a result, so that in fact the core of
Sherborne is Victorian as well as medieval.
There are now about 650 pupils at the school.
The abbey church was repaired in the
fourteenth century following a fire, and
embellished in the following century with
spectacular fan vaulting that visitors nowadays
come from far and wide to see.

MAIDEN CASTLE, Dorset

Just outside Dorchester lies the spectacular
prehistoric earthwork of Maiden Castle. Built
during the Iron Age, it covers 130 acres in all
with ramparts and ditches up to 50 feet deep
and views of the surrounding countryside for
miles around. The site, inhabited since Neolithic
times, was fortified over the years between
about 350 BC and 100 BC, and would have
housed thousands of people in wooden huts, as
well as their animals. The archaeologist Sir
Mortimer Wheeler supervised excavations in the
1930s, which revealed a mass grave in which
the British defenders of the castle were buried
after Roman forces had stormed the ramparts in
about AD 44. A pit full of slingstones was also
found. The Romans seem to have had some
interest in the fort, building a temple here in
the fourth century. But it is thought that
Maiden Castle was probably deserted quite
shortly afterwards, perhaps within another
hundred years. Its massive remains have stood
here, high on the downs, in solitary splendour
ever since.

RIVER EXE, Devon

The River Exe rises high on Exmoor, near the north coast of Devon, but winds its way south through the county before reaching the sea. Many places on its route are named after it – Exford, Exton, Exebridge, Up Exe, Nether Exe and of course the county town, Exeter. A few miles downstream it finally meets the sea, and Exmouth has grown up on the eastern bank of the estuary. This small town might have become a fashionable resort had it found itself on one of the early railway lines, but the South Devon Railway was built on the other side of the river. By the time Exmouth got its own railway it was too late, and the town remained popular only with Exeter holidaymakers. It had one great advantage over other seaside towns east of the estuary, however, and that was its sandy beaches – all the others are shingle. On the western side of the Exe, in the foreground of the picture, lie the small villages of Starcross and Cockwood, with the railway line from Paddington to Penzance running alongside the river, no more than a few feet from the water.

DARTMOUTH, Devon

The Royal Naval College at Darmouth turns its back firmly on inland Devon and faces out to sea, across the small town lying below it. This massive building was constructed in the early years of the present century as a school for naval officers to replace the training ship HMS *Britannia*, whose name it still bears. The present Duke of York was a student officer here three-quarters of a century after his great-great-grandfather, King Edward VII, opened the college in 1905. It was designed by Sir Aston Webb, whose other buildings include London's Victoria and Albert Museum, the Admiralty Arch at one end of The Mall and, at the other end, the new façade that was added to Buckingham Palace in 1913. Dartmouth is an appropriate place for such a college, since it was an important military and civil port for many centuries. The English contingent for the Second and Third Crusades assembled here in 1147 and 1190 respectively, and there was a thriving trade in cloth and wine. But eventually ships grew too large for Dartmouth's restricted harbour and now it is primarily known as a yachting centre. And a very beautiful place for sailing it certainly is, with its picturesque old houses clinging to the steep hillsides and the well-wooded banks of its estuary providing a fine backdrop.

THURLESTONE ROCK, Devon

This extraordinary, almost architectural rock stands just off the South Devon coast near the small village of Thurlestone. The coast here has become popular with holidaymakers, but their arrival is a very recent phenomenon compared with the existence of Thurlestone Rock itself. Proof that it has looked much the same for many centuries lies in the fact that the village is named after it: Thurlestone means 'pierced stone'.

RIVER ERME, Devon

The people of South Devon are blessed with one of the most beautiful stretches of coastline in England. Rolling green fields and woods reach right down to the water's edge and there are fine, clean estuaries for bathing and sailing. The landscape has fewer trees now than in times past, but otherwise is still remarkably unspoilt, and nowhere more so than the Erme estuary. The river runs down from Dartmoor through an area of rich farmland known as the South Hams, until it reaches the sea near Mothecombe. Here, the beach is a popular place in summer with those who know their way to it along the deep, narrow lanes.

DARTMOOR, Devon

Dartmoor is one of England's last great wildernesses. By international standards it is very small, covering only about 365 square miles, but its central uplands are still untamed by man, and the marks left by history can be clearly read. Its granite tors rise to just over 2,000 feet above sea level: here, at Holwell Tor (in the foreground) and Hay Tor, they are about 1,500 feet up. From the bracken-covered hilltops it is possible to see many miles across the surrounding Devon countryside. In this case the south coast at Torbay, thirteen miles away as the crow flies, is just visible beneath the alternately dark and dazzling sky. Dartmoor (a national park since 1951) and its near neighbour, Bodmin Moor in Cornwall, are the first areas of high land encountered by rain clouds blowing in from the south-west, and suffer heavy rainfall as a result. But the benefits of such a climate are plain to see in the lush green cleaves and steep valleys that run off the edge of the moor.

SPEKE'S MILL MOUTH, Devon

In sharp contrast to the gentle estuaries of the South Devon coast, North Devon presents a bleaker face to the onslaught of the Atlantic. Here at Speke's Mill Mouth, near Hartland Point, there are rocky expanses instead of sandy beaches, and bare fields instead of wooded slopes. But the coastline is as rewarding to explorers as its southern counterpart. There are waterfalls and rock pools, and dramatic clifftop footpaths from which the small island of Lundy is sometimes visible, far out in the sea. North Devon has a variety of popular coastal towns and villages, but the concentration of buildings and people evaporates only a short distance inland and there are only rolling fields and old farmsteads as far as the eye can see.

PLYMOUTH, Devon

The mouth of the beautiful River Tamar is
known as the Hamoaze. On one side (the left in
this picture) lies the city of Plymouth, in the
county of Devon. On the other is Cornwall, for
the river forms the boundary between the two
along almost its entire length (it rises only
about three miles from the north coast). Until
1859 the only way of crossing the river here was
by ferry, and one of the oldest routes is still in
use today across the narrow stretch where the
river flows into Plymouth Sound. In 1859
Brunel's railway bridge, a little farther
upstream, introduced trains to Cornwall; it was
opened by Prince Albert. The suspension road
bridge next to it was not completed until 1961.
Plymouth is a city of about 250,000 people
nowadays, but for a long time it consisted of
three separate towns, one of which became the
Royal Naval Dockyards, seen here in the top
left-hand corner of the photograph (and now
privatized). The yards have been the birthplace
of many of England's great ships, but this made
it the focus of intensive German air raids during
the Second World War and central Plymouth
was razed to the ground.

PLYMPTON, Devon

Devon has been the birthplace of many painters,
but her most celebrated native artist is
undoubtedly Sir Joshua Reynolds, who was born
here at Plympton St Maurice in 1723. His father
was master of the grammar school, whose
cloister was drawn by the young Joshua and
which still survives, as can be seen clearly here.
Reynolds began his career as an artist by
painting portraits of naval officers and their
families at nearby Plymouth, before moving to
London where he became the first president of
the Royal Academy in 1768. The people of

Plympton chose him as their mayor in 1773 but
otherwise were extremely slow to pay tribute to
their most famous son, finally placing a
memorial in the church in 1904. The little town
is now almost surrounded by the suburban
sprawl of Plymouth, but its pleasant old
buildings perpetuate some of its former
character, giving some idea of the lively place it
once was when it boasted a castle, a weekly
market, four fairs and important status as a
stannary town – one of four in Devon licensed to
collect duty on the tin mined on Dartmoor.

CALSTOCK, Cornwall

This handsome viaduct spanning the River Tamar at Calstock carries one of the few little branch lines in England to have been left open by British Rail. The train carries passengers from Gunnislake, just north of here, through Calstock and down to Plymouth every morning and brings them home again at night. The journey takes about twenty minutes, and it is at Calstock that the train passes from Devon into Cornwall. The Tamar valley is known for its crops rather than for its railway, however, and Calstock is at the heart of the local flower- and fruit-growing industry. Its numerous glasshouses can be seen plainly here. They benefit from the south-facing slope of the village, and there are many more on nearby hillsides. The climate in this sheltered valley is mild and sunny, and crops such as daffodils and strawberries are common, with 'pick-your-own' enterprises that are popular with local people. Calstock receives waterborne visitors too, since the Tamar is navigable this far inland.

ST ANTHONY HEAD, Cornwall

The lighthouse at St Anthony Head guards the eastern point of the entrance to Carrick Roads – the name given to the great inlet beside Falmouth into which several rivers flow. The Roads provide deep sheltered water for ships that dwarf the trees standing on the adjacent wooded slopes, and at Falmouth itself there is one of the deepest natural harbours in the world. This little lighthouse was built in 1835, and stands sixty-five feet above the sea. Like the other lighthouses in England and Wales (there are about a hundred) it is controlled by Trinity House, which takes its name from the Trinity Guild established in the thirteenth century by the Archbishop of Canterbury. Until the sixteenth century most of its lighthouses were built of wood. In exposed positions, even stone lighthouses did not last long until the problem of their design was solved by John Smeaton, a London clockmaker. His pioneering lighthouse for the Eddystone Rock, about twelve miles off Plymouth, was built in 1759 and now stands on Plymouth Hoe.

Launceston is a small place by modern standards, but in the Middle Ages it was Cornwall's main town, with a castle and a priory. Nowadays it has housing estates and a bypass as well, and is neglected by visitors on their way to the coast. This is just as well, because the narrow streets and crowded marketplace make it unsuitable even for local traffic, which has to reach the centre via a stone arch in the old town wall. The castle lost its military role several centuries ago, though part of it was later used as a prison – among others for George Fox, founder of the Quakers, when he was arrested here in 1656. Another famous visitor, Thomas Hardy, arrived here on the train in 1870 on his way to St Juliot, near Boscastle. At that time he was still a practising architect and had been sent to Cornwall to make drawings of St Juliot's church preparatory to its restoration – some of his sketches are still kept in the church. While there he met the rector's sister-in-law, Emma Gifford, whom he married four years later, and on whom the heroine of his early novel, *A Pair of Blue Eyes*, is based.

RESTORMEL CASTLE, Cornwall

Restormel Castle was first built on a hill above the River Fowey by the Normans, and was complete by the thirteenth century. The architectural historian Sir Nikolaus Pevsner called it 'the most perfect example of military architecture in Cornwall, and in its plan one of the most consummate of England'. From the air its clean, grey-and-green symmetry makes it look more like a child's toy than a massive stone edifice with walls eight feet thick and a moat thirty feet deep. It has been owned by the Dukes of Cornwall since the fourteenth century, but it fell into disuse long ago: visitors who saw it even in Elizabethan times wrote of its decay. Nowadays it seems remarkably complete for its age, and is open to the public.

RIVER CAMEL, Cornwall

The sands of the Camel estuary are much appreciated by thousands of children – and adults – every year, but they have not helped the local port of Padstow. Irish boats sailed up this river many centuries ago, trading fish and wine with the town, which is just off the left-hand side of this photograph. But the river is slowly silting up, and the spit of sand at its mouth is so notorious that it has earned itself the name of Doom Bar. Legend recounts that the bar began to form after a mermaid threw sand at a boy who had tried to shoot her. Then the railway arrived in Padstow in 1899, winding its way along the side of the estuary from Wadebridge, and took yet more business away from the sea. There are still fishing boats in Padstow, however, and the place thrives now as a tourist attraction, together with its neighbour across the river, the small sailing centre of Rock. The disused railway track is now a footpath. Sir John Betjeman used to come to this part of Cornwall for holidays and he thought the ride alongside the estuary one of the most beautiful train journeys he knew.

QUANTOCK HILLS, Somerset

The Quantock Hills are Exmoor's lesser-known but no less lovely neighbour. They stretch from a point just north of Taunton almost to the North Somerset coast, where the village of East Quantoxhead, in the foreground of the photograph, lies between them and the sea. Small villages shelter in the coombes on the east and west flanks of the hills, and surrounding fields peter out as the land rises steeply to a height of 1,260 feet, where bracken and moor grasses hold sway. This was the landscape that influenced the Romantic poets Samuel Taylor Coleridge and William Wordsworth when they came to live here in the 1790s. Coleridge was the first to arrive with his wife and baby, moving in 1796 to a cottage in Nether Stowey, a village on the eastern side of the hills just off the left-hand edge of this photograph. William Wordsworth and his sister Dorothy moved from Dorset in the following year in order to be near him, and rented Alfoxton Park, a house near Holford which is now a hotel. It stands among trees in the left-hand middle distance of the picture.

GLASTONBURY TOR, Somerset

An unusual view of Glastonbury Tor makes the steep climb to the top look like an easy stroll. There was a time when the Tor was one of only a few patches of high ground in a sea of marshland, for this part of Somerset is known as the Levels, and much of it is no higher than sea level. Were it not for locks at the mouths of the rivers, the sea would still drown the fields at high tide, and even man-made barriers and drainage schemes cannot prevent some flooding during heavy rainfall. Glastonbury is renowned for its historical associations. Legend records that Joseph of Arimathea visited the place, and some say he was accompanied by the boy Jesus. Glastonbury's famous thorn tree is supposed to descend from one planted by Joseph, and it is also said that the Holy Grail is buried somewhere beneath the Tor. Joseph is alleged to have built a chapel which was the foundation of the great abbey whose ruins can be seen in the town. Later, runs the legend, King Arthur and his queen, Guinevere, were buried here: monks living at the Abbey claimed to have discovered their bones in an old graveyard.

WELLS, Somerset

Wells, with a population of only 9,000, is England's smallest cathedral city. The presence of this beautiful building indicates its former importance and has helped make it one of the most attractive places in Somerset. The cathedral dates from the twelfth century, and is famous for its breathtaking west front decked with statues that originally would have been painted and gilded. It also has a fine octagonal chapter house, to which the Vicar's Close, a street of medieval houses, is connected by a covered bridge, just visible on the far right of the picture. Some say this was built to keep the clergy dry; others take a more sceptical view, believing that it was built to protect them from the anger of the townsmen during one of those town-versus-church disputes common in cathedral cities. By the fourteenth century, Wells was the most important centre in the county, and some fine houses were built over the centuries. Several of the best buildings are occupied by the cathedral school. The town has expanded in recent years, but there can be few country towns in England where buildings as historic as the cathedral and bishop's palace still abut farmland as they do here.

CHEDDAR GORGE, Somerset

Craggy rocks and plunging gorges are perhaps more often associated with the landscape of northern England, but they are to be found in parts of the south too, and particularly here at Cheddar. This is the most dramatic and best known of Somerset's outcrops of mountain limestone, though there are others elsewhere on the Mendip Hills. The gorge has been created by the action of water, which dissolves limestone and leaves great crags exposed as the valley wears down. Underground streams have also worn channels through the rock and created caves that are eerily decorated with deposits of stone left behind by evaporating water, forming stalactites and stalagmites. It is no wonder that the area is popular with potholers. But they are by no means the first humans to have seen the Mendip caves: there is evidence to suggest that the area was inhabited during the last Ice Age.

BRISTOL, Avon

Bristol is a thriving, busy city of nearly half a million inhabitants, with a university, docks that were once known the world over, an expanding business community and a spectacular gorge. In the days when ships sailed here up the Avon the town built its prosperity on trade, in particular the slave trade, memories of which live on in the names of streets: Blackboy Hill, Whiteladies Road. Nowadays the ships have gone – apart from SS *Great Britain*, which is permanently moored here and open to the public – and houses and offices have been built on the old quays. The city was bombed during the Second World War and is now lumbered with the ugly concrete Broadmead shopping centre; but fortunately the Georgian crescents and terraces of Clifton escaped damage. They start just behind the crescent-shaped City Hall, climb up and down Brandon Hill (at top left of the photograph) and continue to the suspension bridge. To their right are the buildings of Bristol University, including the large tower of the Wills building visible at the top of the long straight road, which is actually quite a steep hill. It is named after the Wills family who were generous supporters of the university in its early days.

BATH, Avon

Bath was already a popular watering-hole when the architect John Wood the Elder settled there in 1727, but it is his building schemes rather than the spa waters that have made the city famous. He proposed a rebuilding of the town centre; but the council gave this idea an unenthusiastic response, so he settled instead for the development of the Barton estate just to the north. The Circus was built as part of that development between 1754 and 1758. It is one of the best-known places in the city, a perfect circle of five-storey houses faced with golden Bath stone – rivalled only by Royal Crescent, built by his son John Wood the Younger. The city's heyday lasted throughout the eighteenth century, though in those days its numerous and fashionable visitors came to take the waters and to enjoy the 'season' rather than to admire the architecture. The fact that the city still possesses many of its handsome terraces and parades is due in part to the decline of its importance in the nineteenth century, when high society started to visit the Continent again after the disruption of the Napoleonic Wars. Now Bath is prized as England's best example of a Georgian city.

SEVERN BRIDGE, Avon

The slender outline of the Severn Bridge in the
ethereal evening light belies its enormous
strength. Its elegant frame is capable of
supporting streams of thundering vehicles as
they cross the estuary that separates England
and Wales; the only restrictions being on those
weighing more than 200 tons. The bridge,
whose main span measures 3,240 feet, was
designed by Sir Gilbert Roberts and was opened
in 1966. Until then, the southernmost road
connecting England and Wales was at
Gloucester. Nowadays motorists take the easy
motorway route across the bridge for granted –
except when winds are so strong that traffic is
reduced to single file or, in exceptional
circumstances, denied access altogether.

OLD SARUM, Wiltshire

The great earthworks known as Old Sarum were created in the Iron Age as a hill fort, covering twenty-eight acres and commanding a view for miles in every direction. The Saxons chose it as the site for their county town in the early eleventh century and it became an important medieval centre. About 1075 the Bishop of Sherborne in Dorset moved to Old Sarum and built a cathedral, followed by a moated castle. The lines of the cathedral are still clearly visible in the ground, though its stones have long since disappeared. Now that the site is deserted it is hard to imagine that a small town ever stood here. And yet it might well have lasted into the twentieth century like other medieval settlements, had it not been for persistent arguments between its ecclesiastical and military communities, plus the fact that it suffered from a shortage of water. Eventually Bishop Poore packed up and moved a couple of miles to the south, where he laid the foundation stone for Salisbury Cathedral.

SALISBURY, Wiltshire

However fine a cathedral may have looked on the hill of Old Sarum, it is hard to imagine it being more beautiful than the one that was built instead in New Sarum, otherwise known as Salisbury. This must be one of the most visited buildings in the country – and with good reason, for its situation, on the edge of a charming city and beside the gentle River Avon, is what everyone expects of an English scene. This one has hardly changed since John Constable painted his famous picture of it in 1823 for his friend the bishop, and Anthony Trollope in the 1850s found it the inspiration for the first two books in his Chronicles of Barsetshire. It is sometimes difficult to remember that the cathedral close has looked as it does today for a comparatively short time: for many centuries it was surrounded by a graveyard that was tidied away only when Bishop Shute Barrington called in the architect James Wyatt in the 1780s. Wyatt created the expanse of grass that suits the building so well; and the houses that frame it make the finest cathedral close in the country.

WESTBURY WHITE HORSE, Wiltshire

England has a number of white horses carved into its chalky hillsides. Some of them are very old but this one, at Westbury, dates only from the eighteenth century. Passengers on the Paddington to Penzance train get a good view of it as they fly past. It seems a pity that the horse is not making more of an effort to fly too, for its placid stance is rather tame. But the Westbury horse was tampered with by the Victorians, who no doubt felt that a quiet and correct demeanour was only fitting in such a public place.

STONEHENGE, Wiltshire

Stonehenge is a gigantic, mystical remnant of a long-forgotten civilization, standing alone on Salisbury Plain with only prehistoric burial mounds for company. Our familiarity with huge buildings has dulled our reaction to these massive stones, and the need to cope with thousands of visitors has drastically affected the setting. How different Stonehenge must have looked only a century or two ago, let alone in prehistoric times when this part of Wiltshire appears to have been particularly important to early Britons. They began work at Stonehenge c. 2800 BC, but continued to extend and rearrange the monument over several centuries. Bluestone was brought from the Preseli mountains in Dyfed by sea and river, then overland. Huge sarsen stones, each weighing twenty to thirty tons, were transported from the Marlborough Downs; a feat that experts reckon must have taken at least ten years. Stonehenge may be a temple, or an astronomical observatory, or both – but it is certainly not what it is claimed to be by latter-day 'Druids'. The popular connection between the stones and Celtic priests was first made in the seventeenth century by the antiquary John Aubrey.

WINDSOR CASTLE, Berkshire

This building must rank high in the list of most famous castles in the world. Windsor Castle has played a prominent part in England's history ever since it was founded by William the Conqueror. Its present familiar form is made up not only of early buildings but of extensive alterations made less than 200 years ago by Sir Jeffry Wyatville for King George IV. At its upper end are the state apartments, while below the tower is St George's Chapel with its stalls of the Knights of the Garter. Legend has it that the Order was founded at Windsor by King Edward III after he retrieved the fallen garter of the Countess of Salisbury and countered the suggestive comments of courtiers with the declaration 'Honi soit qui mal y pense' – which became the motto of the Order. Windsor figured largely in the life of Queen Victoria, for it was here that she met Prince Albert, here that she proposed marriage to him and here that he died of typhoid in 1861. During the First World War Albert's German surname, Saxe-Coburg-Gotha, was dropped and the Royal Family assumed the thoroughly English name of Windsor.

MILTON KEYNES, Buckinghamshire

The Open University at Milton Keynes is Britain's largest university, but not a single one of it's 150,000 students attends this campus. Instead, they receive tuition through the post and via television and radio. This excellent method of teaching, which makes study possible for thousands of people who cannot attend conventional courses, began in 1969 when the university was established here at Walton Hall – the eighteenth-century hall itself can be seen at the centre of the campus. All the other buildings have sprung up during the last nineteen years. It is a large place because 2,000 people work here, even though there are no students: the staff, 800 of whom are academics, are busy with the making and writing of courses and programmes and with the administration of the system. Their students range in age from sixteen to ninety or more. To ensure that there is some human contact, the university also runs local study centres all over the country.

OXFORD, Oxfordshire

There is nowhere in England quite like Oxford. Its pattern of college quads, spires and gardens create a unique atmosphere. In the heart of Oxford there is a timelessness about the golden stone walls and in the lanes that run between them, and of course in the fact that these buildings have been used for the same purpose for centuries. No one quite knows why the medieval market town of Oxford became the home of one of the world's greatest universities; the colleges seem to have evolved in the twelfth century after King Henry II ordered students home from the Continent, and numbers grew rapidly. The townspeople became so irritated that in 1355 a battle erupted in which sixty-two students were killed. Relations between 'town and gown' have been rather quieter since then, and Oxford has grown into a sizeable city with many interests besides the university, particularly car manufacture in the suburb of Cowley. This view is taken looking north-west, with the High Street running diagonally across the left-hand side, the domed Radcliffe Camera and Bodleian Library in the centre, and New College and The Queen's College in the lower right-hand corner.

HENLEY, Oxfordshire

Henley stands gracefully on the banks of the
Thames, surrounded by that river's grandest
rural scenery: green water meadows, great
hanging woods and long views that are
reminiscent of paintings of the Romantic era.
The town has the familiar, comfortable air of
one that grew prosperous in the sixteenth,
seventeenth and eighteenth centuries but
missed the industrial revolution. No great
factories or main railway stations crashed into
its pleasant streets; no sudden expansion of
population devoured its surrounding fields and
engulfed its old high street. Nowadays it is near
enough to London to be swamped by day
trippers, and many houses have been built in
the area. But Henley has made few concessions
and its entertainments are traditional ones:
boating and teashops are its specialities. Its
famous Regatta was first held in 1839, inspired
by a race between rowing crews from Oxford
and Cambridge that had taken place two years
previously, and is a highly popular excuse for
dressing up and enjoying a garden-party
atmosphere – regardless of the unpredictable
weather.

DIDCOT POWER STATION, Oxfordshire

The power station at Didcot is a well-known
feature in the landscape of this part of England.
The Central Electricity Generating Board has
done a good deal of landscaping on the site in an
effort to diminish the impact of its buildings –
but the six cooling towers, each one 426 feet
tall, cannot help but be prominent in the gently
undulating countryside of south Oxfordshire.
The station was built between 1965 and 1970 on
the site of a former Army ordnance depot and is
one of eighty-one power stations producing
electricity in England and Wales. The stockpile
of coal in the foreground arrives from the East
Midlands coalfield in 1,000-ton trainloads. Some
idea of the scale of these massive buildings can
be gained when one learns that the two groups
of cooling towers are half-a-mile apart.

STOW-ON-THE-WOLD, Gloucestershire

The market square in Stow is a distinctive place, even from 2,000 feet up. The town grew up on the road known as the Fosse Way, which the Romans built from Cirencester to Lincoln, and has been a marketplace for centuries. Nowadays its chief trade – apart from the business of accommodating its many visitors – is in antiques, many of which find their way across the Atlantic after leaving Stow. You don't have to be an antique-hunter to enjoy the town, however. Many people come to look at its buildings and to use it as a base for exploring the Cotswolds. Others pay it a visit only when its famous horse fairs are held, when nothing could be farther from their minds than furniture and forays into the hills, and horses alone hold sway.

LOWER SLAUGHTER, Gloucestershire

Lower Slaughter is one of the most visited places in the Cotswolds. Originally it formed a single village together with its near neighbour, Upper Slaughter, but they split into two a long time ago. Both are small places, made picturesque by the Cotswold stone used in the construction of their houses and their situation on the banks of the little River Eye. New buildings are made of local stone in order to harmonize with the old, a practice widely used in the Cotswolds.

WARWICK CASTLE, Warwickshire

Warwick Castle is pre-Conquest in origin, but it was greatly altered in the nineteenth century. Under the present ownership of Madame Tussaud's it is the late Victorian period that dominates the private apartments. In 1978 the castle was sold by the then Lord Brooke, son of the seventh Earl of Warwick, and some of its contents were dispersed in an auction that created quite a controversy. The family removed their own private possessions from their living quarters and Madame Tussaud's was left with a number of empty rooms. After two years of research, and at the expense of £250,000, it recreated in waxworks one of the house parties that were held at the castle during the lovely summer of 1898. The Prince of Wales – later

King Edward VII – is there, as is his son, also the Duke of Marlborough, Lady Randolph Churchill and the young Winston Churchill, along with many others. The waxworks convey the atmosphere of those last great extravagant years of the nineteenth and early twentieth centuries, before the Great War irrevocably altered the lives of the British aristocracy.

SYMONDS YAT, Hereford & Worcester

The Wye is a beautiful river, and at Symonds Yat it is perhaps at its most spectacular. It turns so sharply that for a while it flows due north, even though the point at which it enters the Severn estuary is directly to the south.

Then it loops right back on itself, almost making an island of the land inside the loop, and enters this marvellous wooded gorge. On one side is Herefordshire, on the other Gloucestershire, and about a mile ahead is the border with Wales. The Gloucestershire that borders the Wye here is very different from the one familiar to admirers of the Cotswolds. There are no honey-coloured buildings and no upland landscapes, for the country here is forest – the Forest of Dean, an ancient coalfield that must be the prettiest in the country. Symonds Yat means the pass, or gate, of Symond; it was inhabited in Roman times, when it must have made a fine look-out point, 500 feet above sea level with views in every direction.

MALVERN HILLS, Hereford & Worcester

The great line of the Malvern Hills surges up out of the flat Severn Valley, making a landmark that can be seen for miles in every direction. Farmers of the past have edged their boundaries farther and farther up the slopes but the top is too steep and bare for agriculture to take hold, and so the Malverns are still wild at the summit. This is some of the scenery that inspired the great English composer, Sir Edward Elgar. He was born in a cottage at Broadheath, near Worcester where his father had a music shop, and lived in a succession of houses in the area between that city and the Malvern Hills. Sometimes he moved to London, but his home country always drew him back. He loved to be beside the River Severn and the Teme, and to contemplate the hills that are said to have inspired his *Caractacus* and *Enigma Variations*. He died in 1934 and was buried alongside his wife in the churchyard of St Wulfstan's in Little Malvern.

MALVERN, Hereford & Worcester

Malvern, like Stoke-on-Trent (see page 83), is a town made up of six different places though, unlike the towns of Stoke, these all share a common name. Great Malvern, North Malvern, Malvern Link, West Malvern, Malvern Wells and Little Malvern all lie near the extraordinary spine of the Malvern Hills, and Great Malvern is chief of the six. This photograph shows its town centre with the church, which is all that remains of a monastery, and the theatre and Winter Gardens below it, next to the park. Malvern came comparatively late to the role of a fashionable English spa but attracted public attention in the 1840s because of its hydropathic establishment, opened by two doctors, which was the first of its kind in the country. The Victorians built their rather gaunt grey stone houses in the town, and it became immensely popular. Its reputation lives on, in a faded sort of way, with the retired community it attracts, and with its large number of schools, the best known of which, Malvern College, was established during the town's Victorian heyday.

RIVER SEVERN, Hereford & Worcester

This handsome lock lies not on a canal, as one might expect, but on the River Severn on the southern outskirts of the city of Worcester. The lock house stands on a small island in the river not far downstream from the cathedral, and near the site of the famous Battle of Worcester, which took place in 1651 and from which Prince Charles – later King Charles II – escaped into Shropshire. There, at Boscobel, he hid from his enemies in an oak tree that has provided inspiration for the naming of countless public houses ever since.

MADRESFIELD COURT, Hereford & Worcester

The name Madresfield means 'the field of mowers', a phrase conjuring charmingly romantic visions of hot summer days before the invention of tractors and hay-baling machines. Madresfield Court's immediate surroundings have been made rather too formal to admit of that particular pretty picture, but one can easily imagine the dignified and leisurely life that was no doubt enjoyed beside its moats and among its carefully tended topiary. Formal gardens often look their best from the air, and these are certainly striking. The house originated in the Tudor era and is the ancestral home of the Lygon family, who became Earls of Beauchamp. It was greatly altered and extended by them in Victorian times. Tucked away behind it, an intricate maze makes a pattern just visible beyond the trees.

MUCH WENLOCK, Shropshire

This photograph was taken above the small town of Much Wenlock, looking north to the Wrekin, the great hill that dominates the landscape in this part of Shropshire. The county is about the same size as Wiltshire, but far less known, full of beautiful, sparsely populated stretches of countryside and dramatic hills that rear up in sudden ranges, as if they felt they must prepare the traveller for the even more dramatic mountains that lie ahead in Wales. Much Wenlock is built on a contrastingly miniature scale, in brick and stone and timber, with narrow streets and tiny shops; the ruins of

its old priory are the largest thing about it. Until recently its nearest urban neighbours were Wolverhampton away to the east and Shrewsbury to the north-west, but now the new town of Telford is spreading across the fields beyond the Wrekin.

THE WREKIN, Shropshire

Here is the Wrekin itself, running south-west towards more Shropshire hills and the mountains of Wales. In between lies the valley of the River Severn, a river that starts life far

away in the Cambrian Mountains above Aberystwyth and winds its way north into Shropshire before turning down through the border country towards the sea. It passes many mountains before reaching the softer southern country, but this one is special: legend has it that the Wrekin was created when a giant accidentally dropped a spadeful of earth on his way to dam the Severn at Shrewsbury. He was certainly a giant, for the mound of earth he dropped stands 1,334 feet above sea level and reputedly provides a view of seventeen counties from its summit.

BIRMINGHAM, West Midlands

Here is the centre of Birmingham, often referred to as England's second city – though there are one or two other places that would no doubt vigorously dispute the title. An agricultural town sited so near the coalfields of the Black Country was bound to feel the effects of the industrial revolution; and it certainly did. Birmingham grew wealthy and, unlike some less fortunate places, was considered sufficiently important by its Victorian merchants and industrialists to be given a number of handsome civic buildings. Some of these have survived, though they have been hemmed in since by much larger blocks so that their human scale has been lost, while Birmingham has become

what is without doubt the most tangled concrete jungle of overpasses and underpasses in the entire country.

WOLVERHAMPTON, West Midlands

Strange it is to think that this vast conurbation was once a scattered collection of small villages. Here is modern Wolverhampton, a tangled mass of concrete and brick and roads and railway lines, its suburban sprawl straggling imperceptibly into other once-distinct towns. The sight prompted J.B. Priestley to write: 'The places I saw had names, but these names were merely so much alliteration: Wolverhampton,

Wednesbury, Wednesfield, Willenhall and Walsall. You could call them all wilderness, and have done with it. I never knew where one ended and another began.' That was back in the 1930s, and the modern visitor might be tempted to say that nothing had changed; but that would be unfair to Wolverhampton, which has at least some vestiges of a separate identity. It was, after all, a medieval market town, and it takes a lot to eradicate a market town completely. Nevertheless, the local coalfields and iron ore industry that were exploited so successfully during and after the industrial revolution have left terrible scars, as well as the enduring name of the 'Black Country'.

BELVOIR CASTLE, Leicestershire

Belvoir Castle (pronounced Beever) stands on one of the oldest country house sites in England. There has been a castle here since Norman times, but after several rebuildings the present structure is far more extravagant than the original would have been. It was designed for the Duke of Rutland by James Wyatt in the early nineteenth century and completed after his death by the Duke's chaplain. Its castellated turrets and towers, like Peckforton's (see page 87), were designed to imitate those of a medieval fortress, so that the castle on its prominent hilltop would make an imposing site; while its interior was equipped with all the comforts available to the aristocracy in the early 1800s. There is no doubt about its striking situation, for it dominates the Vale of Belvoir and makes the surrounding trees seem small.

EDITH WESTON, Leicestershire

Until 1974 England had a county called Rutland. Now that county is officially nonexistent – but its name is perpetuated in Rutland Water, a huge reservoir that was created in the early 1970s in the valley of the River Gwash (now in Leicestershire). In the foreground of the picture is the small village of Edith Weston, and near the far end of the peninsula stretching out into the lake is the equally diminutive Upper Hambleton. There used to be three Hambletons – Upper, Middle and Nether – but the last two are now beneath the surface of the reservoir. What Rutland lost in countryside, however, it gained in a beautiful expanse of water and in the water sports that suddenly it could provide. As this photograph shows, sailing is now a popular sport in landlocked Leicestershire.

STOKE-ON-TRENT, Staffordshire

This sprawling conurbation is made up of six towns that were joined in 1910 under the name of Stoke-on-Trent. Local people still distinguish between Tunstall, Burslem, Hanley, Stoke, Longton and Fenton, but for visitors it is often simpler to think of the place as 'the Potteries'. Clay has been worked here for centuries, but the industrial revolution enabled pottery to be made on a grand scale and created many famous names, of which the best known is probably Wedgwood. In the world of literature the city is known as the birthplace of Arnold Bennett, who portrayed the Potteries as the 'Five Towns' in novels such as *The Old Wives' Tale* and *Clayhanger*. He was born in Hanley in 1867, and the house to which he later moved with his parents is now the Arnold Bennett Museum. His birthplace, like so much of the six old towns, no longer exists.

TAMHORN PARK, Staffordshire

To many people, Staffordshire seems a mainly industrial county. In fact it is largely agricultural, as at Tamhorn where this picture was taken. For centuries it was mainly pastureland but, like many other counties, it has seen acres ploughed up for the cultivation of wheat in recent years. It is a far cry from the situation in the fourteenth, fifteenth and sixteenth centuries, when villages here and all over England were deserted because of famine, plague or – ironically enough – the conversion from arable to pasture or parkland. Tamhorn was one of these vanished villages, lying midway between the old cathedral city of Lichfield (birthplace of Dr Johnson) and Tamworth.

KINDER SCOUT, Derbyshire

Kinder Scout is the highest hill in the Peak District, rising to 2,088 feet at the summit, which is covered with peat bog. Near the highest point the River Kinder rises and escapes the rocky heights by plummeting 100 feet down a cliff. This waterfall is known as the Downfall, but in a high wind sometimes seems to be flowing uphill, so great is the amount of spray given off by the torrent of water. Kinder has been a popular place with hill walkers for many years and has an important place in their history, for it was the scene of a 'mass trespass' in 1932, when a crowd of people pressing for easier public access to the hills deliberately invaded the grouse moors of Kinder. The Peak District National Park was not created until 1951 but it was the first of ten national parks and a suitable vanguard: not only does it extend into six counties, but it lies near vast urban populations. Only 38,000 people live within its boundaries but about 17 million live within fifty miles, and many of them come to the park for recreation.

COWN EDGE ROCKS, Derbyshire

The Peak District of Derbyshire is the name given to the southern end of the Pennine Hills, the great range that runs through England like a spine. In the southern half of Derbyshire there are small stone villages and rounded hills but here, at Cown Edge Rocks not far from Glossop, limestone has given way to millstone grit and the hills are hard and bleak – though even here they have been cultivated by generations of farmers. Only the craggy scarps, or 'edges', have escaped their attentions. Cown Edge is near the northern extremity of the Peak District National Park and only a few miles from Greater Manchester, but a world away in atmosphere.

LOSE HILL, Derbyshire

Lose Hill and the valley of the River Noe are seen here in winter. The village of Edale is just out of sight on the right; Mam Tor is in the distance on the left and the valley is stopped by great hills at its head, where the river rises. This area is just within what is known as the High Peak – millstone grit country, as opposed to the softer limestone landscapes of the Low Peak to the south. One might imagine from its name that the Peak District would include mountains such as are found in the Lake District (see pages 96–101), but the name refers to the area's seventh-century inhabitants, not to its hills. These people were called Pecsaetans, which means hill dwellers, and they must have led a remote existence. For many, life in the Peak District is still too remote, even in the late twentieth century; but others enjoy being able to leave work in the large towns that surround the Peak District and come home to unspoilt dales and uplands.

PECKFORTON AND BEESTON CASTLES, Cheshire

These two castle-topped hills make a strange sight in the midst of the Cheshire plain. One might imagine that both were given fortifications in the Middle Ages as a defensive measure against pugnacious Welshmen, but one of these castles is an impostor. Peckforton, in the foreground, was designed by the architect Anthony Salvin in the 1840s for John Tollemache and was nothing more than a private house; though it faithfully echoed the style of a medieval castle with its moat, portcullis and crenellated walls. Tollemache owned an estate of more than 35,000 acres and was created a baron in 1876. His family's reign at their magnificent home was brief, however. There have been no Tollemaches at Peckforton for more than fifty years and the family recently put their castle up for sale. Beeston Castle, on the other hand, about a mile beyond Peckforton in this picture, is the real thing. It was built early in the thirteenth century, before Wales was finally subdued by England, to guard against Welsh incursions. Its purpose long since obsolete, it has been a ruin for many years.

WIDNES, Cheshire

Industrial Cheshire looks positively ethereal in
the heavy fog of a winter morning, with only
one or two of its tallest buildings piercing the
white blanket. Beneath the fog lies the River
Mersey, with the town of Widnes on the right
and Runcorn on the left; Liverpool is somewhere
far in the distance. Cheshire is certainly a
county of contrasts. Not only does it have the
edge of the Peak District within its boundaries,
the strange humpy hills of Beeston and
Peckforton rising from its dairy pastures, and a
prosperous stockbroker belt south of
Manchester, it is also the heartland of Britain's
important chemical industry. A chemical factory
first opened in Widnes in 1847 and the business
grew rapidly, supplied with coal for power from
the nearby Lancashire coalfields and with salt –
for the production of soda – from the Cheshire
salt mines. It was from this Cheshire chemicals
industry that the great ICI conglomerate
sprang, and Cheshire remains its base.

LIVERPOOL, Merseyside

The setting of Liverpool, on the banks of the
Mersey estuary with that grand view of the sea,
seems naturally to invite trade with distant
shores. The merchants of Liverpool grew
wealthy on trade with America and the port
spread farther and farther along the river.
When that business declined, ocean liners filled
the docks instead and stately edifices were built
along the shore: the Royal Liver Building with
its two distinctive towers, and the Mersey
Docks and Harbour Board building (in front of
the former in this photograph). The city and its
buildings have recently become the focus of
attention from many different quarters, from
government ministers to community
architecture groups, and have been fought over
by political parties of all descriptions. Now the
dock area is beginning to be rehabilitated as a
residential quarter, on the lines of the now-
fashionable dockland of London, and there are
hopes that Liverpudlians will regain some say
in what happens to their city.

GRANADA TELEVISION STUDIOS, Manchester

The adjoining sites of Granada Television and the Greater Manchester Museum of Science and Industry are a scene to gladden the eye of anyone concerned with the life of inner cities, for they are full of activity. The old brick buildings in the centre of the picture are part of the museum and were built originally to house Manchester's first railway station. They now hold a variety of exhibits, including an electricity gallery and a display of 'underground Manchester'. Between these buildings and the canal at the top of the picture is Granada's street set for the series *The Adventures of Sherlock Holmes*, and to its right are the Granada offices, workshops and studios. In front of these is a diminutive row of small red-brick houses that is the set for the unfailingly popular serial *Coronation Street*.

RIVER BOLLIN, Greater Manchester

The little River Bollin pursues a meandering course as it flows through countryside near Manchester Airport. For some miles it forms a wiggly boundary between Greater Manchester and Cheshire before joining the River Mersey at Warrington. Its source, however, is up in the hills east of Macclesfield, on the edge of the Peak District. It certainly sees a variety of landscapes in its short journey to the sea.

BLACKPOOL, Lancashire

This must be the most famous sea front in England. Blackpool is a name that has earned a place in history as being synonymous with the archetypal English seaside holiday. And even though it is often cheaper nowadays to spend two weeks on the Costa del Sol than in one of this country's coastal resorts, Blackpool still retains something of the atmosphere that has made it legendary. There are entertainments by the score – dance halls, boating lakes, golf courses, pleasure gardens, piers and zoos – and of course the Blackpool Tower, built in 1891 to designs by Monsieur Eiffel, whose even better-known Eiffel Tower in Paris this one vaguely resembles. Nor must one forget the sands themselves, acres of them, and the sea – which is almost always very cold. Blackpool was favoured by local gentry and prosperous manufacturers from the late eighteenth century onwards, and enjoyed immense popularity once the railway arrived in the mid-1800s. Nowadays such people are more likely to arrive in the town in order to attend one or another conference, hosted by Blackpool's large hotels.

LANCASTER, Lancashire

Lancaster lies some way north of the grouping of industrial towns with which people tend to associate the county of Lancashire. To the east are high moors, to the west are the sands of Morecambe Bay, and only a short distance to the north is the Lake District. Lancaster was once the chief port in the county, when ships trading with the West Indies used to sail up the River Lune. It was soon overtaken in importance by Liverpool but its old buildings serve as a reminder to its past, and it now has a modern university and new industries to carry it into the twenty-first century. The domed building in the foreground of this picture is known as the Ashton Memorial; it was built here by a local benefactor of that name for the townspeople, in a hilltop park overlooking the town, between 1907 and 1909.

LAXEY WHEEL, Isle of Man

The scale of this water wheel at Laxey, on the Isle of Man, would not disgrace the most sophisticated modern funfair. With a diameter of 72 feet 6 inches, in its heyday it was capable of pumping water from the local lead mines at a rate of 250 gallons per minute. The mines flourished from about 1750 onwards, but the wheel pump was not built until 1854. At the time the wheel itself was said to be the largest in the world and it still draws visitors from far and wide.

CASTLETOWN, Isle of Man

Small, grey-blue Castletown is solidly built of a local Carboniferous limestone that has hardly weathered at all over the centuries: the castle, which was built in 1350, shows only the slightest signs of age. The Isle of Man, on which it stands, was ruled by Norse kings and then by Scots before becoming English in the Middle Ages, and Castletown was its capital until 1862. In that year government was transferred to Douglas, ten miles up the road. It does not take long to reach anywhere on the island since it is only about thirty miles long. Its southern tip lies level with Lancaster while the northern point is about as far north as Whitby. But the trip to the mainland takes some time, unless you fly from the airport: the ferry journey to Liverpool or Heysham lasts nearly four hours. What the island may lack in communications, however, it probably makes up for by its low income tax, which consistently attracts new residents from across the sea in England.

ISLE OF WALNEY, Cumbria

The most southerly point of Cumbria has little in common with the inland area with which the county is usually associated. This is the Isle of Walney, a long narrow spit of flat land stretching from Barrow-in-Furness to the lighthouse in this picture. The view is taken looking west; in the opposite direction are the treacherous sands of Morecambe Bay. Walney is connected to the mainland at Barrow by a bridge, and the town has spread across it; Vickerstown was built on the island to house workers at the Vickers shipyards for which Barrow is famous. But Walney was inhabited long before the dockers arrived. Flints have been found that indicate that the first settlers here were Mesolithic peoples.

BORTREE TARN, Cumbria

The Lake District in the north-west contains the most spectacular scenery in England. Unlike other countries in Europe, we can boast no great mountain ranges; but fortunately there are still wild areas left on this small island. Inevitably, because it is still a wild place, the Lake District attracts many thousands of visitors and in the summer holidays can seem rather too full of hikers and walkers and trippers. But this aerial photograph does not dwell on the humans no doubt present in the landscape. It is taken looking across Bortree Tarn to Lake Windermere, the most popular of all the lakes; but it gives no hint that its waters are often busy with boats and its shores sprinkled with picnic parties.

BOWNESS, Cumbria

This is the gentle face of the Lakes. Here at Bowness-on-Windermere the slopes are modest, trees abound and boating is a popular pastime. Windermere is the largest lake in the area and attracts most attention from visitors, making Bowness the nearest thing the Lake District has to a resort. But planning controls are strict and keep firm control of the tourist industry, so there are far fewer eyesores here than in some other English holiday towns.

CONISTON WATER, Cumbria

There are several reasons why Coniston Water should be a particularly well-known lake, but one is tragic. For it was here that Donald Campbell died in 1967 while trying to establish a new record for speed over water. His boat is thought to have been travelling at about 320 mph when it somersaulted and killed its occupant. Coniston is deep at its upper end and Campbell's body was never recovered. On a happier note, this is one of the lakes that featured in Arthur Ransome's book *Swallows and Amazons*: Peel Island, just off the little promontory midway down the lake in this picture, was called Wild Cat Island in the story. Ransome stayed at Newby Bridge, at the foot of Windermere, while writing the book. This photograph was taken looking north up Coniston, with the softer hills of the southern Lake District to the east and the start of the central mountainous region to the north, including Coniston Old Man, which rises to a height of 2,635 feet. The Victorian art critic John Ruskin moved to a house called Brantwood on the eastern shore in the 1870s – on the principle that 'any place opposite Coniston Old Man *must* be beautiful'. His home is now a museum.

SCA FELL, Cumbria

The mountains of Lakeland present England's greatest challenge to fellwalkers and climbers. This is Sca Fell, a peak of 3,162 feet and a very tricky climb. It shows the rugged character of the Borrowdale volcanic rock of which these central fells are composed. The Lake District divides into three main sections geologically: in the south are the Silurian rocks, which have broken down into soft, rounded hills covered in woodland. In the central area are these mountains, so bare and craggy that they support very little plant life; and in the north are the Skiddaw Slates, the oldest rock in the district, whose flat layers wear away to give smooth slopes and angular outlines.

SCA FELL AREA, Cumbria

Here are England's highest peaks, the Sca Fell area in central Lakeland. Scafell Pike is the highest of them all at 3,210 feet, and is crowned by the National Trust's memorial to those who died in the First World War. The Trust owns a good deal of the Lake District, including the central fells, six of the main lakes, several lake heads and much of the shoreline, as well as many properties and holiday cottages. They have opened Beatrix Potter's little farmhouse at Sawrey to the public, and have made Wordsworth's birthplace at Cockermouth into a small museum dedicated to the poet. The Lake District has attracted many writers in the last 200 years but Wordsworth, whose native country it was and whose descriptions of it are to be found in so much of his poetry, was probably the most influential in drawing attention to the beauty of the place. In 1951 that beauty was formally recognized by the creation of the Lake District National Park, which covers 880 square miles and is the largest of the national parks of England and Wales.

DERWENT FELLS, Cumbria

Snow can cover the peaks of the Lake District's highest mountains for much of the winter, but it all melts by summer. Here it is covering the Derwent Fells. The photograph was taken between Keswick and Braithwaite looking south with the flatter land near the foot of Derwent Water in the foreground. The River Derwent – the name means white or clear water and has been given to several other rivers too – rises in the highest land in England, just below Scafell Pike. It is not surprising that the Lake District has the heaviest rainfall in the country, with as much as 185 inches per year falling in the central mountainous area. A mere 90 inches is normal in places at a lower altitude such as Grasmere. Wordsworth, who lived for several years at Dove Cottage there, acknowledged the unsettled weather but wrote that 'the showers darkening or brightening as they fly from hill to hill are not less grateful to the eye than finely interwoven passages of gay and sad music are touching to the ear.'

103

BAMBURGH CASTLE, Northumberland

Northumberland is full of castles. This one is at Bamburgh, not far down the coast from Lindisfarne, and is very large. It covers eight and a half acres. Bamburgh is an ancient administrative centre for the county and had a castle back in Anglo-Saxon times. But it was King Henry II who decided that more extensive defences were needed against the Scots. He built a new keep, probably knocking down the village houses in the process since they had clustered around the old castle. The 'new' village, which can be seen inland, is largely the nineteenth-century creation of the Crewe Estate, while the castle itself was also altered extensively in the eighteenth and nineteenth centuries.

HOLY ISLAND, Northumberland

The outcrop of rock on which Lindisfarne Castle stands is not particularly imposing, but it is a distinctive feature in the flat, windblown landscape that surrounds it. On this tiny patch of land known as Holy Island – a mere three and a half miles long – there is only a small village, the ruins of a priory, and the castle. The remoteness of the place is complete when the tide is high, for then Holy Island's road to the mainland is submerged beneath the sea. St Aidan must have walked across the sands at low tide when he came here from Iona in 635 and founded a community of monks. In the early years of this century Edward Hudson, founder of the magazine *Country Life*, and his architect Sir Edwin Lutyens transformed the old castle into a beautifully simple, comfortable home. It is now owned by the National Trust and open to the public, who can also visit the pretty walled garden that was built for Hudson across the fields (centre right in this picture) and in which, amazingly, many plants survive the chilly climate. The three small huts below the castle were made from upturned boats.

WARKWORTH, Northumberland

The town of Warkworth, tucked into a bend of the River Coquet, makes a charming picture. Aerial photography may not show the steepness of the hill leading up to the castle, but it gives a marvellously revealing view of the plan of the medieval borough, which was founded in about 1200. Houses were built on either side of the main street and their plots can clearly be seen behind those on the left-hand side, stretching back to a footpath that was the original boundary of the settlement. Many houses were rebuilt in later centuries, but there were no pressures for expansion or change, so the pattern has remained the same. Fortunately, twentieth-century houses have been built beyond the castle, well outside the old centre. The town is protected at its southern end by the great bulk of the Percy family's castle, and at the northern end by the medieval fortified bridge (now bypassed by the 1960s road bridge beside it). It is a traditional, scarcely changing scene that is one of England's most valuable, though increasingly rare, possessions.

LADIES SKERRS AND BUCKET ROCKS, Northumberland

Below the old ramparts of Berwick-upon-Tweed lie these strangely formed rocks. Known as the Ladies Skerrs and Bucket Rocks, they would once have been composed of domes and folds, but the sea has planed them down into great swirling ribs, with little pools that retain water when the tide recedes.

HADRIAN'S WALL, Northumberland

Hadrian's Wall stretches for seventy-three miles across the lonely expanses of upland Northumberland and Cumbria from Wallsend, Newcastle, to Bowness-on-Solway, a few miles north-west of Carlisle. Here at Sewing Shields, about 1,000 feet above sea level, the modern road parts company from the wall as the latter marches past Broomlee and Greenlee Loughs in the distance, on towards the sea. The wall was the northern outpost of the Romans in England, built to repel enemies and marauders from the north, and must have been a bleak posting. Building began in about AD 122 and the work was formidable: the wall was to be twenty feet high, including battlements, and protected along its entire length by ditches and defences on either side. There were seventeen forts scattered along it and a milecastle, or lookout post, every Roman mile (slightly shorter than ours). Yet all this work took the Romans only about five years. At first they built the eastern end of the wall in stone and the western section with earth, but later they rebuilt the latter with stone too. Much of the wall remains 1,860 years after it was completed.

TYNEMOUTH, Tyne & Wear

The medieval priory of Tynemouth looks strangely out of place in the midst of the suburbia that has engulfed this stretch of England's coast. There was no problem with neighbours when it was first built, back in the seventh century, and even in the eighteenth century the place was still remote, until it was realized that north-easterners could have their own seaside resort instead of visiting those of other regions. The Napoleonic Wars were the making of many English watering places, since they prevented people from travelling to the Continent. Tynemouth gained some elegant Georgian terraces and crescents and later, in the Victoria era, the railway arrived and the resort area spread up the coast, through Whitley Bay and Cullercoats. These days, people prefer sea bathing in the Mediterranean to a dip in the North Sea, and the area has become a sprawling dormitory for Newcastle.

NEWCASTLE UPON TYNE, Tyne & Wear

Newcastle is a city of bridges. Two carrying railway lines and two more carrying roads appear in almost any well-known view of the place, with the broad River Tyne flowing below. Newcastle's origins lie in one of the forts built by the Romans on Hadrian's Wall, but its great prosperity was founded on coal shipping, and later on shipbuilding, for which yards were built farther upstream. Its old houses used to huddle together on the steep slope between the castle and the river, but many of them were swept away during construction of the railway station in the 1840s, and more have disappeared in the present century. A grand design for the redevelopment of the city centre was devised not, as one might imagine, in recent years – though there has been a good deal of modern rebuilding – but in the 1830s. Three local men, one the town clerk, another an architect and the third a developer, combined to create great civic buildings that were worthy of Newcastle's prosperity. Since then Newcastle has experienced the very opposite of that prosperity, but it is still an important place for the region.

CONSETT, Co. Durham

The 800 acres on which Consett's gigantic steel works once stood is the largest reclamation site in Europe. The buildings have now gone, the slag heaps are being landscaped and the plan is to replace them with parks, industrial units, housing and leisure facilities of various kinds. New industries have also been attracted to the town because of its status as a development area and they produce a variety of goods, from food to microcomputers. At its peak the steel industry employed 6,000 people here and at the time of closure, in 1980, there were 3,500 who lost their jobs. But since that time another 3,500 posts have been created by the newly arrived companies. Soon there will be few signs of the steel industry that began here in 1840 and dominated the town for so long. Diversification is now the name of the game in order that Consett will never again be so dependent upon a single employer.

DURHAM, Co. Durham

The view of Durham Cathedral, standing high above the River Wear and its tree-covered banks, is renowned. The old city of Durham has a beautiful site, and later changes have not spoilt it. The shape of the narrow hill, surrounded on three sides by the river, has forced development to happen elsewhere over the centuries, and the fact that some of the old buildings on the hill are within the cathedral precincts has no doubt helped to preserve them. Inside the cathedral itself are the tombs of St Cuthbert, whose body was brought here from Lindisfarne after Viking raids, and of the Venerable Bede, who lived at nearby Jarrow. It was in order to house St Cuthbert's body that the cathedral was begun in 1093. But it became the seat of the powerful prince-bishops of Durham, whose importance and quasi-military status derived from their situation in the crucial meeting-ground between the kingdom of England and hostile northerners. Nowadays this part of the city is besieged only by visitors and students, the latter because Durham has a well-regarded and very popular university.

BISHOP AUCKLAND, Co. Durham

The vehicles may be engine-driven instead of horse-drawn, the stalls may sell toys made of plastic rather than wood and there may be rock music in place of a barrel organ; but a fairground is still the gaily festive scene it long has been. And the colours and patterns of its tents and awnings, even of its lorries and caravans, seem all the brighter from the air. Here at Bishop Auckland it seems that the fun has not yet begun or the green playing field would not look quite as pristine as it does.

HIGH FORCE, Co. Durham

This is the well-known waterfall on the upper Tees known as High Force. The river starts its life a few miles farther north, high on the Pennines nearly 3,000 feet above sea level. At its source it is in Cumbria and for a short distance it forms the boundary between that county and Durham; then it flows into Cow Green Reservoir and out over the waterfall known as Cauldron Snout, by which time it is well and truly in County Durham. To see the amount of water that can pound over these great rocks at High Force, you would think that quite a sizeable river was raging here. But the Tees has a long way to go before it widens out and slows down in the softer countryside near Darlington. Above the falls it is no more than a rushing mountain stream, midway through its course it becomes a gentler river favoured by anglers, and at Teesmouth (page 116) it undergoes a further change, becoming a great, sluggish, grey expanse of water flowing through the industrial scenes of Teesside.

BARNARD CASTLE, Co. Durham

The small town of Barnard Castle is named after a man and the castle he built; the locals refer to it simply as 'Barny'. Barnard, or Bernard, was a twelfth-century member of the de Baliol family who founded Balliol College at Oxford, and he built himself rather an imposing place here, the remains of which still make an impression on anyone arriving along the road below (in the foreground of the picture), beside the River Tees. There are many pretty houses in the town, but far and away the grandest is the Bowes Museum, seen in the background of the photograph. Designed in French château style, it was built for John Bowes between 1869 and 1892 to house his collection, which includes furniture, porcelain and paintings, particularly by French artists. Charles Dickens stayed in the town in 1838 while investigating the rather less elevating subject of cheap boarding schools on which to model Dotheboys Hall in *Nicholas Nickleby*.

TEESMOUTH, Cleveland

Teesmouth is a wholly industrial place. Until the nineteenth century there was nothing but mud beside the estuary of the River Tees, but then a man named Henry Bolckow began to develop what was to become a huge iron and steel industry. He also discovered rock salt and anhydrite in the ground that enabled him to start a chemical works, and the result was the town of Middlesbrough. The river was adapted to meet the needs of industry by having its channel dug deeper and its mud flats reclaimed: more than 1,000 acres have been reclaimed at Seal Sands, near the mouth of the Tees, by the dumping of slag, so that more steel and chemical works could be accommodated. There are still long stretches of beach in the area, as at Coatham Sands on the left in this photograph – but the surroundings are not quite what a beachgoer might expect.

ROBIN HOOD'S BAY, North Yorkshire

The connection of Robin Hood, the legendary medieval outlaw, with this village on the coast of North Yorkshire seems tenuous to say the least. One story relates that he kept a boat here in readiness for an escape, should that be necessary; another claims that he helped the Abbot of Whitby to repulse Scandinavian pirates. But one cannot help wondering how he came to be here, so far from Sherwood Forest. Still, it is a pretty name for a pretty place, perched precariously on the edge of the cliff. There is a sea wall now to protect the village against erosion, but many houses are reputed to have fallen into the sea over the years when there was nothing but a long, crumbling drop between them and the water. The villagers' homes are crowded together on the steep slopes, so close to their neighbours that it is said that smugglers used to escape the excise men by climbing through secret cupboards leading from one house to another, from the bottom of the village to the top. When they were not smuggling, the residents of Bay Town (as it is known locally) were out fishing for herring or even whales, or trading as far afield as the Baltic.

MALHAM COVE, North Yorkshire

This part of Yorkshire derives its appearance from the limestone on which it lies. Unlike most rocks, limestone is slowly dissolved by water, so over the aeons it has eroded in a characteristic way. In places it has weathered into great cliffs, or into 'pavements' where deep clefts are formed that in some places lead to potholes and caves. Here at Malham Cove the process has created a huge natural amphitheatre with 300-foot-high cliffs through which the little Malham Beck cuts a path down to the valley.

FOUNTAINS ABBEY, North Yorkshire

The great Cistercian monastery at Fountains, near Ripon, was one of the most important in the country at the time of the Dissolution, when King Henry VIII broke from the Church of Rome and deprived all the monastic houses of their property. Its plate, ornaments and vestments were worth £700 and it owned 4,000 animals. It also possessed a magnificent building, set in a valley to which its founding monks had come from York in the twelfth century. It is hard to believe now that the site must once have been a desolate one, because in the eighteenth century it was absorbed into the Studley Royal park, a picturesque landscape created by its owner William Aislabie. Ruins were considered a great adornment to a landscape at the time and many were built specially for landowners who had none of the genuine variety. Aislabie acquired a magnificent example when he managed to buy the abbey in 1768, by which time it had already been plundered for its stone: some of this had been used to build the nearby Fountains Hall in the early 1600s. The park and abbey are now owned by the National Trust and can be approached along the valley through Aislabie's beautiful gardens.

YORK MINSTER, North Yorkshire

This was the scene in the summer of 1984 after a fire had swept through the south transept of York Minster in July and destroyed its roof. The blaze lit up the night skies and could be seen for miles around. No satisfactory explanation could be found for the fire and so it was declared by some to be divine retribution for the recent, controversial appointment of a new Bishop of Durham. It was by no means the first fire at the Minster, however. The Norman building was almost destroyed by fire in 1137, and the one that replaced it, constructed over 250 years, was set alight in 1829 by a lunatic named Jonathan Martin. Eleven years later there was yet another fire. Miraculously, in spite of this extraordinary history of combustion, the Minster still boasts stained glass from a period spanning the last 800 years. Its south transept is now repaired, with timber donated by several great estates.

YORK, North Yorkshire

York is one of the most popular places on the tourist's English itinerary – small wonder, because it offers a mass of attractions. There is the Minster and an array of interesting old buildings; but there are also museums, city walls, the little shops in the medieval streets, the racecourse and two nearby national parks. It is a handsome old city, awash with flowers in the spring when the banks below the walls are covered with daffodils. This photograph was taken looking east across York and gives a fine view of the thirteenth-century walls, with the Minster rising from the heart of the old quarter. There was a Roman city here called Eboracum, and a Danish one after that, known as Jorvik – hence the famous Jorvik Museum. York prospered in the Middle Ages; the Shambles and Stonegate are the city's two most famous streets dating from this period. In the Castle Museum is a popular reconstruction of local streets at a later period, full of sweet shops and hansom cabs and figures in nineteenth-century costume. York has always been an important place. Its railway station was the largest in the world when it opened in 1877 and British Rail is still a major employer, along with the chocolate factories of Rowntree and Terry.

GLUSBURN, North Yorkshire

This photograph was taken near Glusburn in Airedale, but the pattern of straight stone walls on the hillsides is characteristic of Yorkshire in general. Opponents of changes in farming often claim that the twentieth century is wilfully destroying a timeless landscape, but that argument ignores the fact that, in many parts of England, the landscape with which we are familiar is itself the product of comparatively recent changes. Field boundaries are the prime example. Most of those in the Yorkshire dales are there because of the enclosures of the late eighteenth and early nineteenth centuries, when common land was divided into fields fenced with long straight walls. The most constant factor since then has been the climate, which creates a certain continuity in the landscape simply because the weather is too severe for crops: the only things that survive up here are grass, sheep and cattle – and one or two hardy humans.

CASTLE HOWARD, North Yorkshire

When the late Lord Howard of Henderskelfe, or George Howard as he then was, inherited the family home after the Second World War, it was in a poor state. There had been a fire that destroyed the dome and gutted the south front, and many paintings had been sold. Since then the house has been restored and the gardens filled with a variety of beautiful and rare plants and trees. The original builders of Castle Howard would surely be heartened to see the house and grounds in such fine fettle. These three men – the Earl of Carlisle and his architects Vanbrugh and Hawksmoor – were responsible for the creation of a unique building when they designed Castle Howard in the early years of the eighteenth century. It took decades to build, decorate and furnish, being still unfinished at the death of Lord Carlisle in 1738, by which time he had spent more than £78,000 on the house. The castle is still the home of the Howards and receives thousands of visitors each year, particularly since it was used as the setting for the televised version of Evelyn Waugh's novel *Brideshead Revisited*.

EMLEY MOOR, West Yorkshire

The television mast on Emley Moor, between Huddersfield and Barnsley, soars elegantly into the lowering sky. A view like this, across miles and miles of rich green hills and valleys, makes it easy to forget how overcrowded the small country of England is. Instead of emphasizing the proximity of towns and villages to one another it seems to stretch the acres and sprinkle the population thinly across the countryside. It eliminates scruffy corners and ugly patches and shows us that, in spite of the modern equivalents of 'dark satanic mills', we do still live, in Blake's words, 'in England's green and pleasant land'.

HUMBER BRIDGE, Humberside

It took nine years to build the Humber Bridge, which seems quite reasonable when you consider that it has the longest single span of any bridge in the world: 1,542 yards. Its towers are 533 feet high and the total length of wire in its supporting cables is 44,000 miles. The figures impress; but so does the delicate elegance of the bridge itself, perhaps particularly when lit in this way, by streaks of sun breaking through rainclouds. Even the murky waters of the Humber estuary look beautiful.

SCUNTHORPE, Humberside

A layer of snow may not make industry any more beautiful but, together with the light of a low sun, it certainly helps to create a striking scene. This is Scunthorpe, a centre of heavy industry in Humberside, south of the Humber estuary. Nothing much happened at Scunthorpe until 1859, when beds of ironstone were discovered (though the iron had been worked long before, in Roman times). Ironworks were built in the 1860s, the production of pig iron and steel began, and Scunthorpe's future as an industrial town was settled. British Steel is still a major employer, though many light industries have also been established here in recent years.

HOTHAM, Humberside

The farmland of what used to be the East Riding of Yorkshire, but has been Humberside since 1974, is fertile now thanks to centuries of drainage work by its farmers. There was a time when this was marshland, but reclamation began in the Middle Ages and now almost every square yard is under cultivation. The straight field boundaries are the result of eighteenth-century enclosures, which replaced the old open fields and common land with regular fields and individual farmsteads. This picture was taken above the village of Hotham, where the eighteenth-century field patterns are broken up by remnants of the older fields and the wooded park of seventeenth-century Hotham Hall.

127

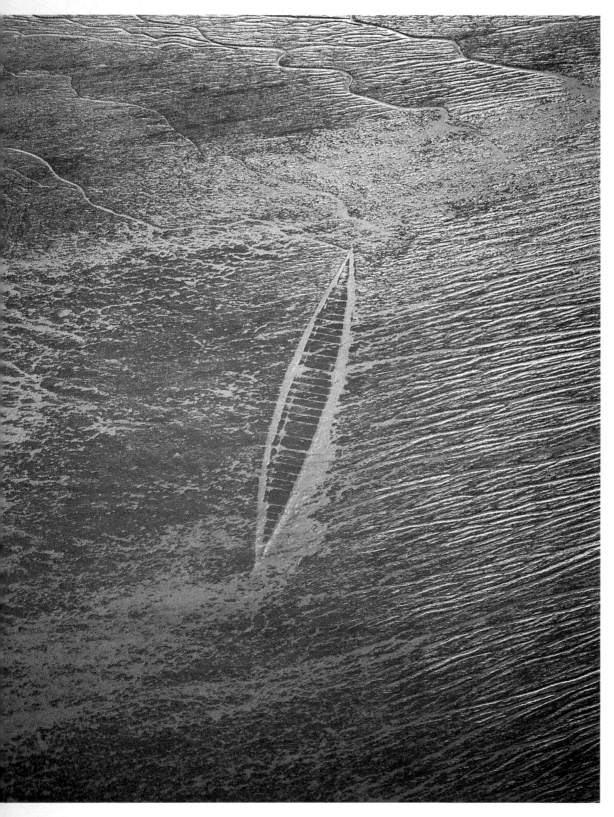

SPURN HEAD, Humberside

A flight over the sea unexpectedly reveals the outline of a wreck lying on the sandy floor of the ocean. This ship's hull probably dates from the end of the last century, or the early years of the present one. There is no sign on the lower deck beams revealed here that it ever contained an engine, so it is probably the remains of a wood or steel schooner. Only the bottom of the hold remains, below the level of the stern, which is why there are points at either end.

WILLOUGHTON, Lincolnshire

The fields near Willoughton provide a good example of a modern man-made landscape. There is rich soil in Lincolnshire, and its farmers have made sure that not a square inch of it is wasted. Fields are of a size convenient for the latest machinery, and crops are those that fetch high prices, either on the open market or because of the 'intervention' prices of the European Community. Over the last few years, farming land like this has been a profitable business, though it is possible that a combination of surpluses and conservation pressures may bring changes. What, one wonders, would the nineteenth-century labourers who fought against the introduction of farm machinery, because of the threat it posed to their livelihoods, make of such a landscape? It is intensively cultivated, certainly, and by farmworkers, but very few of them are required to create such a scene: just one or two behind the wheel of phenomenally sophisticated machines.

STAMFORD, Lincolnshire

The handsome grey-gold stone of which
Stamford is built also gave the town its name:
'Stamford' means a stone-paved ford. The town
stands in Lincolnshire, but only just, for it is at
the junction of several counties. In the days
before the boundary reorganization of 1974 it
was next door to England's smallest county,
Rutland, but now that county is officially nonexistent and it is bordered only by
Leicestershire, Northamptonshire and
Cambridgeshire. While tourists have flocked to
the better-known Cotswolds, Stamford and its
stone-built neighbours in old Rutland have kept
a low profile; but latterly the expansion of
Peterborough, not far away, has created a
booming house market as newcomers 'discover'
this beautiful place. The charm of prosperous
English market towns is enduring: these were
the places where merchants had their fine
homes and where local landowning families
built their town houses. Through luck and a
history of sympathetic town planners, those
buildings are still there for us to enjoy today.

LINCOLN, Lincolnshire

Lincoln is still a remarkably unspoilt old hilltop
city, with delightful buildings gathered round
the cathedral, interspersed with gardens and
trees as all good townscapes should be. The
cathedral is largely a product of the period
1192–1232, a comparatively short space of time
in which to construct such a building in the
Middle Ages, and is the third largest cathedral
in England (only York Minster and St Paul's are
larger). It possesses some particularly fine
misericords, and a collection of early printed
books in the colonnaded library, a building
added by Wren (just visible to the left of the
chapter house). The precincts lack a bishop's
palace because it was damaged in the Civil War
and its stone later used to repair the cathedral:
its remains can be seen in the bottom left of the
picture. There was once a wall running right
round the cathedral close, but all that now
remains of it is the fourteenth-century
Exchequer Gate, opposite the twin towers of the
cathedral's west front.

WEST BURTON, Nottinghamshire

A distant view of the West Burton power station, near the River Trent at Bole, disguises its vast size. It is said that St Paul's Cathedral could be fitted inside one of its eight cooling towers and the Central Electricity Generating Board is hoping to add three more, even larger towers, to an adjoining site. The central boiler house is as high as a twenty-storey office block. Each day the station uses 19,000 tonnes of coal and the sixty-acre stock ground can hold up to 2 million tonnes in case of emergency.

COLSTON BASSETT, Nottinghamshire

The medieval church of Colston Bassett, a village between Nottingham and Grantham, was abandoned at the end of the last century when a new church was built in the village. Five of its bells were taken across to its successor, and the font was removed. Now poor old St Mary's is well and truly a ruin, with grass growing in the nave and weeds where the altar once stood. Its isolation is emphasized by the arable farming that surrounds it, leaving it marooned in its overgrown little churchyard.

CLEY NEXT THE SEA, Norfolk

There is still a customs house and a quay at Cley next the Sea, but no longer enough water on which to steer a boat. This small village used to be nearer the sea than it is today, but in 1823 a bank was built that pushed back the water with the result that grass now grows in the harbour and marshland has silted up the creek. The lack of a harbour is not a disadvantage to modern Cley, however. Even without one it is a popular place with visitors who come to the north Norfolk coast for the sort of healthy, bracing summer holidays that English people still enjoy, in spite of the ease of foreign travel.

NORWICH, Norfolk

Norwich is a city of churches. There are still thirty-two medieval ones left. Norfolk was a densely populated and prosperous area in the Middle Ages, and as a market town and main centre for the region, Norwich grew prosperous too. It had a thriving textile industry and a fine cathedral, and was one of England's most important towns until the time of the industrial revolution, when other places began to overtake it. Norfolk became a place remote from the mainstream of industrial England; but now the city is again reasserting itself as East Anglia is becoming established as one of the country's main growth areas. In the cathedral close pictured here, however, the hurly-burly of modern life seems far away. The cathedral is built of Caen stone and its spire is second only to Salisbury's in height. The lovely collection of buildings that surround it date from every major building period in English history. Nearby, new houses are being built on the banks of the River Wensum to help accommodate all the people who want to live and work in this city.

SANDRINGHAM, Norfolk

The Prince of Wales acquired Sandringham estate in 1861. The sizeable sum of £220,000 was paid out of the accumulated income from the Duchy of Cornwall for the house and 7,000 acres, but it was not considered a very prepossessing place at the time, set as it was in rather bleak heathland near the windswept north coast of Norfolk. Lady Macclesfield, a member of the Princess of Wales's household, thought 'it would be difficult to find a more ugly or desolate-looking place.' But the Prince – later King Edward VII – launched himself enthusiastically upon a programme of improvements to the estate that included tree-planting, road-building, and renovation of workers' cottages and of the main house itself. He also bought another 4,000 acres and extended the estate's sporting facilities so that he could enjoy one of his favourite occupations, shooting. The bag after a day's shooting at Sandringham sometimes reached 3,000 birds, and the game larder there was believed to be one of the largest in the world. Life at Sandringham is conducted on a more modest scale today, but it is still one of the Royal Family's homes, and the church contains many of their memorials.

BURY ST EDMUNDS, Suffolk

The town of Bury St Edmunds bears the same name as its abbey, which was dedicated to St Edmund, the last king of East Anglia, who was killed by the Danes in 869. The abbey was a major place of pilgrimage in the Middle Ages but is now visible only as ruins, and houses have been built into what was once its west front (centre of picture). There has been a series of buildings and rebuildings of the church here: the Norman tower that is still standing served both as a gateway to the abbey and as a bell tower for the church of St James. That church was rebuilt in Tudor times, reroofed 120 years ago by the well-known Victorian architect Sir George Gilbert Scott, and then altered in the present century, when the large chancel was built. St James is the cathedral church of the diocese of St Edmundsbury and Ipswich, but has been so only since 1914, which explains why it does not enjoy the usual dignified position of English cathedrals within a precinct. St James must be one of few cathedrals in England to front so unceremoniously on to the street.

FELIXSTOWE, Suffolk

Felixstowe is the largest container-handling
port in the United Kingdom. In 1987 about
752,000 containers passed through its docks and
its newest development, the Trinity terminal,
can accommodate the largest container ships
afloat. There seems very little these days that
cannot be transported by this method, from
furniture to fruit and vegetables. Bulk liquids
are unloaded at the jetty in this picture: there
are several pipes through which liquids of
various kinds are pumped into storage drums
on shore, some of which can be seen here. The
pipes are made of stainless steel so that they
can be cleaned between being used for liquids as
diverse as diesel fuel and molasses. The picture
shows, however, that the method is not without
fault, for that ominous-looking slick should
surely not be there.

SOUTHWOLD, Suffolk

Many of Suffolk's small towns are remarkably
unspoilt, having escaped the pressures of the
last 200 years that have wrought such changes
elsewhere. Here at Southwold the little streets
of Georgian houses appear much as they must
have done to the genteel visitors who came here
during the summers of the Victorian age. There
are old-fashioned beach huts on the shore below
the modest cliff, a nineteenth-century
lighthouse and a beautiful fifteenth-century
church that was spared when most of the town
was destroyed by fire in 1659. Students of
maritime history will know Southwold as the
place off which the English Navy fought the
Dutch at the Battle of Sole Bay in 1672.

CAMBRIDGE, Cambridgeshire

Disagreements between 'town and gown' in Oxford during the thirteenth century are said to have been responsible for the foundation of Cambridge University. A group of Oxford scholars packed up and moved to what was then a fairly run-of-the-mill market town. The college-building that resulted has made Cambridge one of the most beautiful towns in England. Such an array of buildings is a feast to anyone interested in architecture; but you need no special knowledge to enjoy Cambridge. The beauty of the place is quite apparent to the walker strolling in the Backs – the name given to the riverside land behind the colleges – or to the punter floating along the river. In this photograph, King's College Chapel is prominent in the centre, with Clare College to the left and Trinity College to the left of that, where the river bends. But there is another face to the town, and one which has grown up only in recent years. That is its prominence as a centre for science and technology, which has made it a fast-growing place and a magnet for employment.

BURGHLEY HOUSE, Cambridgeshire

Burghley House, which originally stood in the now abolished county of Huntingdon and Peterborough, is now in Cambridgeshire, and in lovely grounds that were landscaped by Capability Brown. It was built by William Cecil, Lord Burghley, in honour of Queen Elizabeth I, and what a monument to the Elizabethan age it is. Inspired by French and Dutch architecture and probably incorporating Cecil's own designs, it took about forty years to complete. Its exterior is still much as its creator knew it. Inside, however, most of the decoration is the result of work undertaken by the fifth Earl of Exeter in the late seventeenth century, though it was not completed for another century. His descendants still own Burghley, and the estate is now the setting for the famous Burghley Horse Trials, which attract thousands of onlookers each year.

141

ELY, Cambridgeshire

Ely is dominated by its cathedral. In fact, the building looms over the surrounding fenland too. Ely is a market town whose wharves beside the River Ouse (just beyond the photograph on the left) were once busy with the unloading of incoming goods, the river being a vital means of communication in the days before the low-lying fens were drained. This is where Hereward the Wake made his stand against the invading Normans in the eleventh century, amid the desolate and inhospitable marshes. The Normans may have been unwelcome, but they left a great monument in the form of the cathedral; though they were not responsible for its crowning glory, the octagonal lantern. That was added later, in the fourteenth century, after the collapse of the tower they had built above the crossing. The sacrist, Alan of Walsingham, sent for one of the best craftsmen in the country, William Hurley, the King's carpenter, and the octagon that they devised is a triumph of medieval carpentry, its massive supporting timbers hidden so that it appears to be held up only by slender ribbed vaults. A recent donation from Mr Paul Getty has prevented land near the cathedral being sold for development.

ROCKINGHAM CASTLE, Northamptonshire

'Castle' may seem a rather inappropriate name for this lovely old house, since it was long ago rebuilt in a domestic fashion by the Watson family, who continue to live here. But it was originally a Norman fortress, and still has the remains of a keep and a dried-out moat to prove it. Within that moat there are now carefully tended gardens that combine with the warm stone walls to form a tranquil setting – one that was described by Charles Dickens when he used Rockingham as the model for Chesney Wold in his novel *Bleak House*. Dickens was a frequent visitor to the Watsons at Rockingham, and dedicated *David Copperfield* to them. In *Bleak House* his heroine, Esther, says of her first sight of Chesney Wold: 'On everything, house, garden, terrace, green slopes, water, old oaks, fern, moss, woods again, and far away across the openings in the prospect, to the distance lying wide before us with a purple bloom upon it, there seemed to be such undisturbed repose' – though, as readers will recall, there was anything but repose within.

WHISTON, Northamptonshire

There is no shortage of attractive villages in the county of Northamptonshire. This one is Whiston, just outside Northampton itself, standing amid farmland and boasting a rather fine late Perpendicular church. The distinctive yellow-brown ironstone that is found in this part of England was used to build its tower, and makes a bold contrast to the grey, still leafless trees of early spring.

DUNSTABLE, Bedfordshire

Dunstable is a place that has changed greatly in the present century, but the traditional scene of a market under canvas is still to be seen in the town. There is usually an extraordinary variety of goods beneath the awnings of such markets, from sausages to stockings, from bananas to brass candlesticks, but almost always based on a mixture of fruit, vegetables and inexpensive clothing. Business looks fairly quiet on this occasion, but the shadows show that the day is yet young.

AMPTHILL, Bedfordshire

Ampthill is the sort of village that has become
extremely popular as commuters have edged
farther and farther from London, and as the
new 'city' of Milton Keynes has grown up a few
miles to the west. Village homes are usually in
demand at the best of times, and are not always
easy to find in Bedfordshire. Ampthill has some
fine examples, such as the ones in this
photograph. It is interesting to have a view of
the backs of the houses fronting the village
street and to note how the rear of one in
particular fails to keep up the appearance it has
established on its street side (bottom left in
picture). One of its Georgian owners evidently
decided that it must have a classical façade, but
that the back did not matter.

POPPIES, Hertfordshire

Farmers do not like them, but poppies in a
cornfield make a lovely sight. Modern chemical
sprays have eliminated so many weeds from the
agricultural landscape that it is unusual to see
such flowers growing against all the odds.
Poppies are hardy plants: the seeds can lie
dormant for years until a sudden disturbance of
the soil causes them to germinate – which is
why they are so often seen on verges that have
been dug up, or on heaps of spoil on building
sites or at road improvements.

SAFFRON WALDEN, Essex

Saffron Walden is one of Essex's most delightful small towns. Not only does it possess this fine medieval church (the tower and spire were built only in 1831) but it has a magnificent array of domestic architecture, dating from many periods and in several different styles. There are colour-washed cottages, a familiar sight in East Anglia; there are the equally characteristic half-timbered buildings; there are handsome Georgian brick town houses; and there are later Victorian villas. The concentration of such buildings in Saffron Walden's old streets makes it comparatively easy to imagine how the town looked centuries ago when it was thriving on the clothmaking industry. The 'saffron' in its name is an allusion to that industry, for it refers to the saffron crocus which was grown locally for use in the dyeing of cloth and in the colouring and flavouring of food

HARWICH, Essex

Ships sail in and out of the mouth of the River Stour on a summer's evening, on their way to and from Harwich. The ferry in the background, farther upstream, has just arrived from the Hook of Holland, but the ferries go to other destinations as well: Hamburg, twenty hours away, and even Oslo, the journey to which takes thirty-one hours. Ferries have been in business here for many years: the terminus for the Hook of Holland was built in 1894 and ships began to sail to Rotterdam ten years later. But to say they run from Harwich is, strictly speaking, incorrect. The ferry terminus is at Parkston, while the residential area of the town is known as Dovercourt. Harwich, it seems, is a name used more by outsiders than locals.

RIVER BLACKWATER, Essex

For hundreds of years the mud flats of the River Blackwater have been known to Londoners as great wildfowling country. Wildfowling is a minority sport and likely to remain so, since it involves acute discomfort while waiting to get a shot at the elusive wildfowl. Mud and marshes and other cold, wet, windblown places are the wildfowler's natural habitat.

MALDON, Essex

Disused railways tracks are often converted to interesting public footpaths, but walkers have trouble here, just upstream from Maldon, where the old railway bridge has lost its central span. The gap in the middle is useful for small craft, however. Maldon sees plenty of those since it is a popular boating centre, not very far from London and near the main centres of population in Essex.

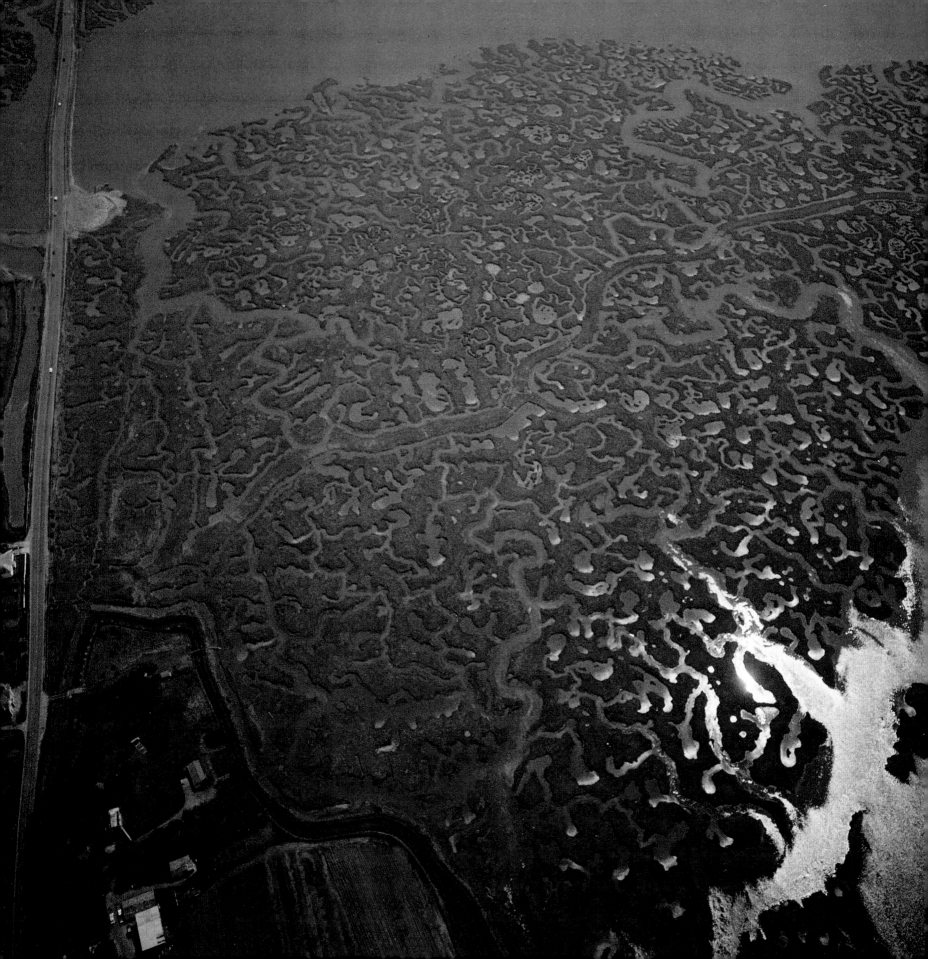

RIVER MEDWAY, Kent

This view shows the former basins and dockyards of the Medway, a famous place in England's naval history. The Navy's association with the Medway towns of Gillingham, Chatham and Rochester goes back 400 years to the time of King Henry VIII, when warships were anchored in the river here for the first time. The dockyards grew to be the most important in the country and nurtured many a famous sailor. Sir Fancis Drake trained here, and Admiral Lord Nelson joined his first ship at Chatham. His celebrated ship HMS *Victory* (see page 26), was launched from this dockyard. But the Navy's presence on the Medway ceased in April 1984 when the dockyards closed and the basins stood empty. Since then, a plan has been drawn up for the redevelopment of the area in the foreground of this photograph – an area that has been given the name of Chatham Maritime. A marina is planned for the basin on the far right, while the one on the far left has become a commercial port. There will be offices, shops and light industry, and the fine old buildings of the dockyard will be preserved.

ST MARGARET'S AT CLIFFE, Kent

This converted windmill stands on the clifftops east of Dover, at a place named St Margaret's at Cliffe. It is enclosed in its little garden by a wall that looks rather like a miniature fortification. The village is not one much mentioned by the guide books; but it must have felt itself horribly in the forefront of events in 1987 when three local men were lost at sea in the disaster of the *Herald of Free Enterprise*, on which they all worked. Since then, the village church has gained a new stained-glass window commemorating the men, as the result of a fund-raising appeal by local firemen.

HOP FIELDS, Kent

Hop fields have been a familiar sight in Kent for centuries, the long rows of poles and wires becoming covered with the fast-growing, pretty vines each summer. Traditionally, the picking of the crop was done by crowds of migrant workers from the East End of London. Hop-growing is still a relatively labour-intensive industry, but has been mechanized nonetheless. Many of the nineteenth-century oast houses in which hops were dried have been converted to homes, and the industry itself has declined. Fewer hops are needed now, since a stronger strain has been developed. The increasing popularity of lager resulted in suitable hops being imported from Germany for a time, but these are now being produced by English growers, either here in Kent or in England's other area of hop gardens, Hereford and Worcester.

LEEDS CASTLE, Kent

Apart perhaps from Windsor Castle and the Tower of London, there is surely no better-known castle in all England, for the picturesque setting of Leeds has undoubtedly made it one of the country's most photographed buildings. It is what people expect a castle to be: romantic, handsomely battlemented and, of course, set exquisitely on an island site – or rather two, for half the castle is on an island of its own, connected to the other by a two-storey covered bridge. It was begun in 857, converted to a royal palace by King Henry VIII and extensively altered in 1822. Then in the 1930s it was restored and used as a home by Lady Baillie, whose elegant decorative schemes can still be seen in some of the rooms. Leeds keeps its visitors amused with curiosities too: there is a collection of dog collars on display in the gatehouse buildings, and the Culpeper herb garden is nearby. The castle has become an important conference centre in recent years.

DOVER HARBOUR, Kent

Dover itself may not be visible in this
photograph, but the scene epitomizes what the
name Dover means to most people. In and out of
the harbour streams one ferry after another,
crossing the Channel to various destinations
with Calais, the nearest, a mere seventy-five
minutes away. The hovercraft in the distance
will get its passengers there even faster, in
thirty-five minutes. This familiar routine is
under threat, however, from the Channel
Tunnel, which is being built nearby. If travellers
take to the underground train that is planned
for the Tunnel, what will become of these
ferries? To future generations this picture may
well appear as archaic as do sepia prints of
horse-drawn vehicles to us today.

DOVER CASTLE, Kent

This spectacular series of buildings at Dover is
crowned by the old castle, 465 feet above sea
level. The sea is just beyond the base of the
white cliff in the bottom left-hand corner of the
photograph, so the picture gives a rather
misleading impression of the steepness of the
site: it is actually quite a climb to the top. On
the way up to the Norman tower of the castle,
the visitor passes not only an ancient church –
St Mary's-in-Castro, built in Saxon times of

Roman materials – but also an even older
building, the Pharos, a Roman lighthouse (right
next door to the church). It must be an odd
sensation to look out over the English Channel
from the top of the castle, with all England
behind you. Dover, at the nearest point to the
Continent and the main gateway to and from
England, has gone down in history time and
again for the impression it makes on those
leaving, and those greeting, English shores.

INDEX